SCHOLASTIC

Building Real-Life
MATH SKILLS

Liane B. Onish

Hi Mom!

Thanks to Sarah Longhi, Mela Ottaiano, Karen Kellaher and to everyone who contributed to this book.

D1530928

Text on pages 3–4 adapted from *Building Real-Life Reading Skills* by Cindy Harris. Copyright © 2009 by Cindy Harris. Used by permission of Scholastic Teaching Resources.

Editors: Mela Ottaiano, Karen Kellaher
Cover design: Jaime Lucero
Interior design: Kelli Thompson
Cover and interior illustrations: Jorge J. Namerow
ISBN: 978-0-545-32964-4
Copyright © 2011 by Liane B. Onish
All rights reserved. Published by Scholastic Inc.
Printed in the U.S.A.

1 2 3 4 5 6 7 8 9 10   40   17 16 15 14 13 12 11

New York • Toronto • London • Auckland • Sydney
Mexico City • New Delhi • Hong Kong • Buenos Aires

Contents

Introduction

Students will sometimes ask, "What's the point of learning this?" or "Why do I need to know that?" You won't hear such comments with this book—because the lessons target real-life situations that connect directly to students' daily lives, both in and out of school. Building real-life math skills gives students a greater understanding of the mathematics they learn in school and helps them apply those same skills to their everyday lives.

What is Real-Life Math?

Real-life math is the math we encounter every day at home, in stores, in school, and in the world at large. It is the math that allows us to accomplish tasks and function as citizens. The real-life scenarios and situations that introduce the units in this book include studying restaurant menus, perusing clothing stores, shopping for groceries, sharing pizza, and planning birthday parties on a budget, to name a few. After tackling these fun and realistic scenarios, students will feel more confident handling money as well as understanding time, distance, and measurement. When students understand how to work with the numbers they encounter in daily life, their mathematical skills and confidence will grow.

How to Use This Book

The lessons in this book are geared toward third-, fourth-, and fifth-graders. Use the lessons in any order as best fits in your curriculum. Lessons can be adapted for whole-class or small-group work.

Teaching Routine

Each real-life math lesson follows the same three-part format:

Teaching Guide: A one- or two-page plan to help you make the most of the lesson.

Let's Work Together: A reproducible introductory activity that you and students use together to explore an example of real-life math.

Now It's Your Turn: A reproducible practice page featuring a similar type of real-life math, so that students can apply their new skills, working independently or with partners.

Teaching Guide

Real-Life Scenario: Each lesson begins with a *Real-Life Scenario* to read aloud—a brief fictional scenario that engages students by giving them a context for understanding the importance of this type of real-life skill. The scenario sets the stage for the lesson.

What's at Stake: This note sums up why math is important to the lesson's scenario. It states the consequences or benefits of using real-life math skills in that context.

Teach: This section takes students step by step through the math they will apply to the *Let's Work Together* activity.

Step 1
Set the stage by helping students connect prior knowledge and experience to build background for the lesson scenario, and introduce the math skills students will use. Step 1 ends with you reading the scenario aloud.

Step 2

Distribute copies of the *Let's Work Together* reproducible to the students and encourage them to think about math skills presented on the page. Step 2 is devoted to reviewing the terminology and operations students will use to answer the questions.

Math terms and vocabulary (numerator, denominator, " = inches, minimum, maximum, and so on) are included for review as needed, as are formulas (l x w = a), and equivalents (12" = 1') where appropriate.

Step 3

Use the guided questions to help students understand and analyze the real-life situation and its component parts. Information is presented in a variety of forms including text, charts, lists, recipes, and maps and other graphics. At the end of the *Teach* section, students will have practiced the math skills they need to apply to *Let's Work Together* and *Now It's Your Turn*.

Challenge: This activity appears in some lessons to challenge students to flex their math muscles a little harder.

Let's Work Together

This reproducible page gives additional information about the real-life scenario, discussed earlier in the lesson. Students use this page to discuss and apply to a real-life scenario the math skills just practiced. *Let's Work Together* can be used with the whole class, small groups, or partners.

Now It's Your Turn

The reproducible activity page gives students the opportunity to apply and practice their math skills. Students can complete this page independently, with partners, in small groups, or as homework. The practice page includes:
- a second model of a real-life scenario that requires math skills;
- questions about the information.

Teaching Guide for Let's Go Shopping! lesson (page 15)

Let's Go Shopping!: One of two real-life math pages included in the lesson (page 17)

The Menu Game

Real-Life Scenario

Every Sunday, Grandpa Herman takes his twin grandchildren, Emma and Ethan, out to lunch. They often go to Grandpa's favorite place, the Midtown Diner.

While they study the menu, Emma, Ethan, and Grandpa like to play Grandpa's Menu Game. To play, they read the menu carefully and estimate the cost of various items they might like to order. Then they use their estimates to give clues—and challenge the other players to guess which menu items they are thinking of!

What's at Stake
Making sure you have enough money for lunch.

Teach

Step 1: Set the Stage
- Ask students to name places they like to go when they eat out.
- Talk about the math skills that can help people figure out what a meal will cost: estimating, rounding up, and rounding down.
- Read aloud the real-life scenario above.

Step 2: Overview
- Hand out copies of page 6.
- Review estimating and rounding up. Explain that when we estimate prices, we round up the price to the next higher dollar if the cents are 50¢ or greater. For example: $1.75 is almost $2.00; $3.89 is almost $4.00.
- Have students round up for these amounts: $2.65, $4.80, $1.95.
- Review rounding down. Explain that when the cents are less than 50¢, we round down to the next lower dollar amount. For example: $1.25 rounds down to $1.00, $4.49 rounds down to $4.00
- Have students round down for these amounts: $3.15, $5.12, $2.35.

Step 3: Guided Questions
Read the menu with students. Ask questions to check for understanding:

❶ How many sandwiches are on the menu? (*four*)
❷ Which sandwich costs the least? How much is it? (*PB&J; $2.95*)
❸ Which sandwich costs around $6? How much is it exactly? (*roast turkey; $5.85*)
❹ Which soup costs about $4? (*lentil*)
❺ Which drinks cost less than $2? How much is each one? (*milk, $1.80; juice, $1.75; coffee or tea, $1.05*)

Let's Work Together
- Introduce Grandpa's Menu Game with these problems:
  —Grandpa says, "I'm thinking of a sandwich that costs more than $4 but less than $5." What sandwich is he thinking of? (*grilled cheese*)
  —Grandpa says, "I'm thinking of a soup and a drink that together will cost about $3." What soup and drink is he thinking of? (*tomato soup and coffee/tea*)
- Work through the problems on the page.

Now It's Your Turn
Distribute copies of page 7 and have students work individually or in pairs to complete the *Now It's Your Turn* activity.

✳ For answers to reproducibles, see page 63.

Name _____ Date _____

The Menu Game

Lunch Specials

SANDWICHES

PB & J $2.95
Grilled Cheese $4.25
Tuna $5.15
Roast Turkey $5.85

SOUPS

Tomato Soup $2.15
Vegetable Soup ... $3.20
Lentil Soup $3.75
Chicken Noodle ... $4.80

DRINKS

Tea or Coffee $1.05
Juice $1.75
Milk $1.80
Hot Chocolate $2.95

Key Math Terms

estimate: to make a rough calculation by rounding

round up: to change a number to the next higher amount (in this case, the next dollar amount)

round down: to change a number to the next lower amount (in this case, the next lower dollar amount)

1. Grandpa says, "I'm looking at a soup that costs about $3."

   What soup is Grandpa looking at?

   _____

   How much does it cost, exactly?

   _____

2. Emma says, "I'm thinking of a sandwich and soup that together cost about $5."

   What items is Emma thinking of?

   _____

   How much will they cost, exactly?

   _____

3. Ethan says, "I plan to get a nice cold milk and some soup. What soup am I thinking of that will bring my total to about $7?"

   What soup is Ethan thinking of?

   _____

   How much would his total be, exactly?

   _____

4. Grandpa says, "I'm thinking of a soup, a sandwich and a drink that together will cost about $14."

   What items is Grandpa thinking of?

   _____

   How much will they cost, exactly?

   _____

Building Real-Life Math Skills • © 2011 by Liane B. Onish • Scholastic Teaching Resources

Name _____ Date _____

The Menu Game

Step 1

Grandpa takes Emma and Ethan to a Chinese restaurant. Read the menu below.

East Meets West
Chinese Food

Appetizers

Egg Roll $1.35
Dumplings $3.95
Spare Ribs $5.25
Popcorn Shrimp $5.65

Fried Rice

Plain Fried Rice $2.25
Vegetable Fried Rice $3.15
Pork Fried Rice $3.65
Chicken Fried Rice $3.75

Noodles

House Special Lo Mein ..$4.95
Beef Lo Mein $5.85
Pork Chow Fun $6.70
Shrimp Chow Fun $7.70

Remember!

Round up to the next higher dollar if the cents are 50¢ or greater. Round down to the next lower dollar if the cents are less than 50¢. To estimate the total cost, add the rounded amounts together.

Step 2

Answer these questions.

1. Emma says, "I'm thinking of an appetizer and a fried rice dish that together cost more than $3 but less than $4."

   What items is Emma thinking of?

   _____

   How much will they cost?

   _____

2. Ethan says, "I'm thinking of an appetizer and a noodle dish that total about $6."

   What items is Ethan thinking of?

   _____

   How much will they cost?

   _____

3. Grandpa says, "I'm hungry for pork chow fun. What appetizer am I thinking of that would bring my total to about $12?"

   What appetizer is Grandpa thinking of?

   _____

   How much will the two items cost?

   _____

4. Pick one item from each menu column that you might like to try. Estimate the total cost of your meal by rounding and adding.

   I would choose

   _____

   Estimated cost

   _____

Going to the Movies

MOVIE TIME THEATER

ADMISSION Child (under 12): $8.50 General: $11.50
Senior (55+): $9.00 ◊ Before noon: 1/2 price ◊ 3-D: All tickets $14.50

It Came From Beyond	1 hr 10 min Rated PG-13 11:45 A.M. 1:15 P.M. 2:30 P.M. 6:00 P.M. 7:30 P.M.
Laugh Out Loud!	1 hr 40 min Rated G 1:30 P.M. 3:30 P.M. 5:30 P.M. 7:30 P.M. 9:30 P.M.
SUPERSTARS! The Musical	2 hr Rated PG 12:15 P.M. 4:25 P.M. 6:45 P.M. 9:15 P.M.
JOURNEY TO MARS 3D	2 hr 10 min Rated PG-13 10:30 A.M. 1:00 P.M. 4:15 P.M. 7:00 P.M. 9:30 P.M.

Real-Life Scenario

Grandma Gloria loves the movies. When she picks up her 10-year-old grandson, Aiden, from school, they walk by the Movie Time Theater to plan their next movie outing.

"I want to see a scary movie, Grandma," said Aiden.

"Me, too," said Grandma, "but let's pick an early showing so I won't have nightmares!"

Outside the theater, Grandma Gloria and Aiden run into the Whitney family, who live across the hall from Grandma. The Whitneys are planning their own movie outing.

"The Mars 3-D movie got interesting reviews," says 14-year-old Nelessa Whitney.

"I might want to see something else," says Mr. Whitney.

What's at Stake
Determining which movie to see and how much it will cost.

Teach

Step 1: Set the Stage
- Ask students to describe the last movie they saw in a theater.
- Talk about the math skills that people use to figure out what time a movie will be over and how much money the tickets will cost: calculating time and money.
- Read aloud the real-life scenario above.

Step 2: Overview
- Hand out copies of page 9.
- Review adding and subtracting time. Remind students that an hour is 60 minutes. When adding time, regroup from the hours to the minutes using 60 rather than 10:

$$\begin{array}{r} 9:15 \\ + 1:55 \\ \hline 10:70 \end{array} \rightarrow \begin{array}{r} 9:15 \\ + 1:55 \\ \hline 11:10 \end{array}$$

Here students will get the answer 10:70. Explain that 60 of the 70 minutes should be moved to the hour side, making the answer 11:10.

- Review operations with money. Remind students that the decimal point separates the dollars from cents:

$11.50 + $8.50 = $20.00
$11.50 x 3 = $34.50
$20.00 ÷ 2 = $10.00
$10.00 − $8.50 = $1.50

Step 3: Guided Questions
Read the movie board with students and point out some of its features (movie running times, start times, prices, etc.). Ask questions to check for understanding.

❶ Which movie has the earliest showing? (*Journey to Mars 3D*)

❷ Which movies have showings before noon? (*Journey to Mars 3D* and *It Came From Beyond*)

❸ How much time is there between the last two start times of *It Came From Beyond*? (*1 hr 30 min*)

❹ Aiden's Grandma Gloria is 57. How much would her ticket to *Laugh Out Loud* cost? (*$9*)

Let's Work Together
Work through the problems on the page.

Now It's Your Turn
Distribute copies of page 10 and have students work individually or in pairs to complete the *Now It's Your Turn* activity.

✳ For answers to reproducibles, see page 63.

Name _____ Date _____

Going to the Movies

MOVIE TIME THEATER

ADMISSION   Child (under 12): $8.50   General: $11.50
Senior (55+): $9.00 ◇ Before noon: 1/2 price ◇ 3-D: All tickets $14.50

It Came From Beyond	1 hr 10 min Rated **PG-13** 11:45 A.M. 1:15 P.M. 2:30 P.M. 6:00 P.M. 7:30 P.M.
Laugh Out Loud!	1 hr 40 min Rated **G** 1:30 P.M. 3:30 P.M. 5:30 P.M. 7:30 P.M. 9:30 P.M.
SUPERSTARS! The Musical	2 hr Rated **PG** 12:15 P.M. 4:25 P.M. 6:45 P.M. 9:15 P.M.
JOURNEY TO MARS 3D	2 hr 10 min Rated **PG-13** 10:30 A.M. 1:00 P.M. 4:15 P.M. 7:00 P.M. 9:30 P.M.

Key Math Terms

time: Hours and minutes are separated by a colon (:) 9:49 P.M. There are 60 minutes in one hour.

A.M.: the hours from midnight to noon

P.M.: the hours from noon to midnight

money: Dollars and cents are separated by a decimal (.) $12.45

1. About how long is each film?

    It Came From Beyond _____

    Laugh Out Loud! _____

    Superstars! _____

    Journey to Mars 3D _____

2. Which movies are under two hours long?

    _____

3. Fifty-seven-year-old Grandma Gloria and 10-year-old Aiden decide to see *It Came From Beyond*. What time is the first afternoon showing of that movie?

    _____

4. Who will pay more to see the first afternoon showing of *It Came From Beyond*, Grandma or Aiden? How much more?

    _____

5. How much will their two movie tickets cost in all?

    _____

6. How much would their two tickets cost if they went before noon?

    _____

7. Nelessa Whitney and her mom want to see *Journey to Mars 3D* at 4:15. Her 8-year-old brother and dad are not interested in that movie. What movie could her dad and brother see that is playing at about the same time?

    _____

8. If Nelessa and her mom go to the 4:15 showing of *Journey to Mars 3D*, about what time would the movie end?

    _____

Name _____ Date _____

Going to the Movies

FILM FESTIVAL
MOVIE THEATER

ADMISSION   Child (under 12): $6.50 ◇ General: $9.50
Senior (55+): $7.00 ◇ Classic Films One-Day Pass: $15
Classic Films Weekend Pass: $25 ◇ Sorry, no discounts for early shows.

Black Beauty
1 hr 35 min Rated PG-13
11:00 A.M. 12:45 P.M. 2:30 P.M. 4:15 P.M. 7:45 P.M.

Treasure Island
1 hr 10 min Rated G
10:30 A.M. 11:50 A.M. 1:10 P.M. 2:30 P.M. 5:10 P.M.

Gulliver's Travels
1 hr 20 min Rated PG
12:00 P.M. 1:30 P.M. 4:30 P.M. 6:00 P.M. 7:30 P.M.

The Three Musketeers
2 hr Rated PG-13
12:15 P.M. 2:25 P.M. 4:35 P.M. 6:40 P.M. 8:50 P.M.

Step 1
One weekend, Grandma Gloria and Aiden decide to check out a theater that shows classic movies. Read the movie board to see what's playing and when.

Step 2
Answer these questions.

1. How much longer is *The Three Musketeers* than *Black Beauty*?

2. Grandma Gloria plans to take her grandson Aiden to see *Treasure Island* on Saturday morning. Then they plan to meet Aiden's parents for lunch at noon. What time do Grandma and Aiden need to see the movie?

3. How much would tickets to *Treasure Island* for Grandma Gloria, age 57, and Aiden, age 10, cost?

4. Grandma Gloria may go back to the theater the same day to see the 4:15 P.M. showing of *Black Beauty*. What time will it end?

5. If Grandma Gloria wants to see two films on Saturday and two more films on Sunday, should she buy a Weekend Pass? Why or why not?

6. Nelessa Whitney and her mom are neighbors of Grandma Gloria. They arrive at the theater at 11:45 A.M. but must leave at 3:00 P.M. They want to see *Treasure Island* and another movie. Do they have time to see another film? If so, which one?

Building Real-Life Math Skills • © 2011 by Liane B. Onish • Scholastic Teaching Resources

On the Field

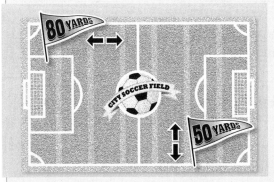

Real-Life Scenario

"It's about time," Coach Rogers said to Coach Evans.

"You are so right," said Coach Evans. "The kids are playing really well. Their skills are excellent, but this field…"

"I know, said Rogers. "The field is a real embarrassment. Thank goodness the city is willing to buy new turf to fix it up."

"I'm glad they asked for our recommendations," added Evans.

"So which of these brands of artificial turf do you like best?" asked Rogers.

What's at Stake
Making sure a soccer field is in tip-top shape.

Teach

Step 1: Set the Stage
• Ask students to share what sports or other extracurricular activities they're involved in, and where they play, perform, or practice. Have them describe the condition of the field, court, pool, studio, or the like. Then ask them to tell how those spaces could be improved.

• Read aloud the real-life scenario above.

Step 2: Overview
• Hand out copies of page 13.

• Review area, the amount of space within a shape, calculated by multiplying length x width: $a = l \times w$

• Review perimeter, the outside border or rim of a shape, calculated by adding the length times 2 plus the width times 2: $p = 2l + 2w$

• Have students use rulers to measure the length and width of classroom desktops or tables in inches. Then have them calculate the perimeter. Next, have them find the area. Remind students that area is expressed in "square" inches, feet, yards, meters, miles, etc.

• Then ask students to imagine that the tables or desktops are going to be refinished. The refinishing cost is by the square inch. If the refinishing costs 29¢ a square inch, how much will it cost for each desk or table?

[*Hint: You might want to suggest that students round up 29¢ to 30¢, multiply by the number of square inches, and then subtract 1¢ per square inch from the total.*]

• If further reinforcement for area is needed, have students cut different-color art paper into one-inch squares. Then have them tape the squares to cover the top of a desk or table. Next, have them count the square inches that cover the surface. Point out that students will get the same answer they would get by using the formula $a = l \times w$. Finally, have students write 29¢ on each square of art paper and then add them up (or multiply by the number of squares) to find the cost of refinishing.

• Review the following units of measure: inches, feet, yards, miles.

> 12 inches = 1 foot
>
> 3 feet = 1 yard
>
> 9 square feet = 1 square yard
>
> 1,760 yards = 1 mile
>
> 5,280 feet = 1 mile

On the Field

Teach continued

- Have students measure your classroom in inches and then convert the perimeter into feet.
- Review conversions:
  inches to feet: divide by 12
  feet to inches: multiply by 12
  feet to yards: divide by 3
  yards to feet: multiply by 3
  square feet to square yards: divide by 9
  square yards to square feet: multiply by 9

Step 3: Guided Questions

Look at the field diagram with students. Ask questions to check for understanding:

❶ What is the length of the soccer field? (*80 yards*)

❷ What is the width of the field? (*50 yards*)

❸ What operation do you use to find the area? (*a = l x w*)

❹ How do you find the perimeter? (*add together the measures of all sides: 2 x l plus 2 x w*)

❺ How could you find the area in square feet? (*You could find the length and width in feet and multiply them together, or you could find the area in square yards and multiply by 9 to convert to square feet.*)

❻ Imagine that you are buying new turf for a soccer field. It is sold by the square foot. How would you calculate the total cost? (*find the area in square feet and multiply that figure by the price per square foot*)

Let's Work Together

- Work through the problems on the page. Have students use calculators if needed.
- You may want to point out that soccer fields vary in size, depending upon the age of the players. Because players spend much of their time running, younger players with shorter legs will get tired more quickly. A smaller field for smaller players means they will run less and have more fun by getting more passes. The soccer field in the diagram is a size appropriate for youth players.

NOTE: For younger students, you may want to round up or down the price per square foot of artificial turf for easier calculations.

Now It's Your Turn

Distribute copies of page 14 and have students work individually or in pairs to complete the *Now It's Your Turn* activity.

✳ For answers to reproducibles, see page 63.

Challenge

Home Game

Have students calculate area and perimeter of the field, court, or studio where they do their favorite extracurricular activity. The school basketball court is one place to start!

Name _____   Date _____

On the Field

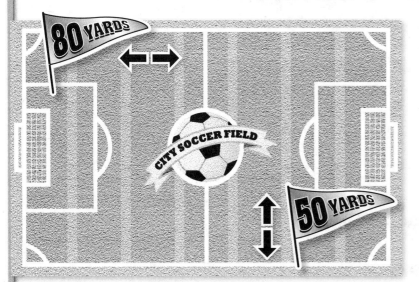

 Remember!

area = length x width

perimeter = (2 x length) + (2 x width)

Key Math Terms

area: the space within a shape

perimeter: the outside border or "rim" of a shape

Look at the city soccer field and solve the problems. The conversions listed below will help you.

1. What is the perimeter of the field in yards?

_____

2. What is the perimeter of the field in feet?

_____

3. What is the area of the field in square yards?

_____

4. What is the area of the field in square feet? [*Hint: Multiply the area in square yards by 9.*]

_____

5. The soccer players often run laps around the field. About how many laps around this field make a mile? Did you use area or perimeter to solve this problem?

_____

BRAND A

BRAND B

BRAND C

6. The city recreation department plans to put new turf on this field. How much will it cost for each brand of artificial turf?

Brand A costs $5.69 per square foot.

It would cost _____.

Brand B costs $4.99 per square foot.

It would cost _____.

Brand C costs $4.89 per square foot.

It would cost _____.

Conversions

3 feet = 1 yard

9 square feet = 1 square yard

1,760 yards = 1 mile

5,280 feet = 1 mile

Name _____ Date _____

On the Field

Step 1
Look at the dimensions of the professional soccer field.

 Remember!

area =
length x width

perimeter =
(2 x length) + (2 x width)

Step 2
Answer these questions.

1. What is the perimeter of this professional soccer field in yards?

_____

2. What is the perimeter of the field in feet?

_____

3. The professional players run laps around their field as part of their warm-up routine. About how many laps around this field make a mile?

_____

4. What is the area of the field in square yards?

_____

5. What is the area of the field in square feet?

_____

6. Imagine that the international soccer agency wants to put new turf on this field. How much will it cost to cover the field in each brand of turf?

BRAND A

Brand A costs $5.69 per square foot. It would cost

_____.

BRAND B

Brand B costs $4.99 per square foot. It would cost

_____.

BRAND C

Brand C costs $4.89 per square foot. It would cost

_____.

Conversions
| 3 feet = 1 yard | 9 square feet = 1 square yard | 1,760 yards = 1 mile |

Building Real-Life Math Skills • © 2011 by Liane B. Onish • Scholastic Teaching Resources

Let's Go Shopping!

Smart Kids Mart

Now 50% off!
T-shirt Was $12

1/2 off second pair!
Jeans Was $24

Now 50% off!
Polka-Dot Sweater Was $20

Now 25% off!
Puffy Parka Was $40

Now 25% off!
Turtleneck Was $16

1/2 off second pair!
Sweatpants $10

Real-Life Scenario

Kendra found a flier in the Sunday newspaper for her favorite clothing store.

"Look, Mom! Smart Kids Mart is having a sale! I need new jeans." Kendra's mom looked at the flier and smiled. "You're growing so quickly! You do need new jeans, and your brother's sweatpants are ready for the rag bag. I guess it's time to go shopping. And we will . . . right after you figure out the sale price of the jeans, sweaters, parkas, shirts, and sweatpants in the flier!"

What's at Stake

Figuring out how much you save when shopping on sale.

Teach

Step 1: Set the Stage
• Ask students to share their favorite places to shop. Discuss how they know if something is a good buy.
• Read aloud the real-life scenario above.

Step 2: Overview
• Hand out copies of page 17.
• Review fractions and percents. Remind students that percents are fractions of 100: 100% = $^{100}/_{100}$, 10% = $^{10}/_{100}$ (or $^1/_{10}$), 50% = $^{50}/_{100}$ (or ½), and so on.
• Write 50% of $12 on the board. Have students name the equivalent fraction ($^{50}/_{100}$), and then rename it in lowest terms (½): $^{50}/_{100} = ^5/_{10} = ^1/_2$
• Have students note that 50% means half. Then write the problem: ½ × $12 = _____. Have students calculate the sale price of 50% (or ½ off) of $12 ($6). Review the steps to find the new price:
—Change 50% to a fraction (½).
—Find ½ of the original price. This is how much money you save.
—Subtract the discount from the original price ($12 – $6 = $6) to find the sale price.
• Repeat for 25% ($^{25}/_{100}$, ¼). Have students calculate 25% of $16 ($4), and the sale price

($12). Then have them tell how they got the answer. Review the steps to find the new price:
—Change 25% to a fraction (¼).
—Find ¼ of the original price ($4). This is how much money you save.
—Subtract the discount from the original price ($16 – $4 = $12) to find the sale price.

Step 3: Guided Questions
Read the prices with students, then ask questions to check for understanding:

❶ What is the original price of the short-sleeve T-shirts? (*$12*)
What is the discount? (*50%*)
What fraction is 50%? (*½*)
What is ½ of $12? (*$6*)
How much do the T-shirts cost on sale? (*$6*)
How much money do you save? (*$6*)

❷ What is the original price of the turtlenecks? (*$16*)
What is the discount? (*25%*)
What fraction is 25%? (*¼*)
What is one quarter of $16? (*$4*)
How much do the turtlenecks cost on sale? (*$12*)
How much money do you save? (*$4*)

Let's Go Shopping!

Teach continued

❸ What is the original price of a pair of jeans? (*$24*)

What is the discount? (*½ off second pair*)

What is half of $24? (*$12*)

How much does the <u>second</u> pair of jeans cost? (*$12*)

How much do two pairs of jeans cost when the second pair is half off? (*$36*)

Let's Work Together

• Review the steps to find a discounted price:
  — Change the percent to a fraction.
  — Find the fractional amount of the original price. This is how much you save.
  — Subtract the fractional amount from the original price to find the sale price.
• Work through the problems on the page.

Now It's Your Turn

Distribute copies of page 18 and have students work individually or in pairs to complete the *Now It's Your Turn* activity.

✳ For answers to reproducibles, see page 63.

Challenge

Average Cost

What is the average cost of a pair of jeans if a person buys two pairs?

Let's Go Shopping!

Name _____ Date _____

Smart Kids Mart

T-shirt Was $12 — Now 50% off!

Jeans $24 — 1/2 off second pair!

Polka-Dot Sweater Was $20 — Now 50% off!

Puffy Parka Was $40 — Now 25% off!

Turtleneck Was $16 — Now 25% off!

Sweatpants $10 — 1/2 off second pair!

1. What is the sale price of a polka-dot sweater?

   _____

2. What is the sale price of a puffy parka?

   _____

3. What is the total for four pairs of jeans at this sale?

   _____

4. What is the sale price of two pairs of sweatpants?

   _____

5. What is the sale price of a turtleneck shirt?

   _____

6. Kendra's family goes to the sale. They buy two pairs of jeans, two pairs of sweatpants, one parka, and one turtleneck. How much do they spend?

Key Math Terms

percent (%): part of 100. $50\% = .50 = \frac{50}{100}$

fraction: part of a whole or a group of things

$\frac{1}{2} =$

$\frac{3}{4} =$

Remember!

Three steps to find a sale price when given a percentage off:

Step 1: Change the percent to a fraction. ($10\% = \frac{1}{10}$)

Step 2: Find the fractional amount of the original price. This is how much you save. ($\frac{1}{10}$ of $10 = $1)

Step 3: Subtract the fractional amount from the original price to find the sale price. ($10 − $1 = $9)

Name _____ Date _____

Let's Go Shopping!

Step 1

Read the flier below.

Step 2

Answer these questions.

1. What is the sale price of a sports T-shirt?

_____

2. How much are two hoodie sweatshirts on sale?

_____

3. How much are two pairs of camouflage pants on sale?

_____

4. What is the sale price on two animal T-shirts?

_____

5. What is the sale price of a striped T-shirt?

_____

6. A family buys two hoodies, two sports T-shirts, and one striped T-shirt. How much will they spend in all?

_____

Building Real-Life Math Skills • © 2011 by Liane B. Onish • Scholastic Teaching Resources

Go, Team!

FOCUS SKILLS:
- Reading a Chart
- Money
- Time

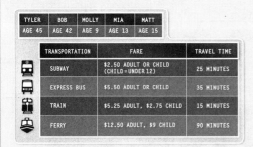

| TYLER | BOB | MOLLY | MIA | MATT |
| AGE 45 | AGE 42 | AGE 9 | AGE 13 | AGE 15 |

TRANSPORTATION	FARE	TRAVEL TIME
SUBWAY	$2.50 ADULT OR CHILD (CHILD = UNDER 12)	25 MINUTES
EXPRESS BUS	$5.50 ADULT OR CHILD	35 MINUTES
TRAIN	$5.25 ADULT, $2.75 CHILD	15 MINUTES
FERRY	$12.50 ADULT, $9 CHILD	90 MINUTES

Real-Life Scenario

Tyler and Bob are cousins and huge Yankees fans. Every year, they take all their kids to a game. Molly (age 9), Mia (age 13), and Matt (age 15) look forward to this outing. Last year, Bob drove. The traffic was a nightmare both ways. This year, they will leave the driving to someone else. Mia did the research and made a chart to show their transportation options.

What's at Stake

Figuring out the best way to get to the game, and what time to leave home.

Teach

Step 1: Set the Stage

- Ask students to name a sporting event they have been to with friends or family members. Talk about who played, who won, and how they got to and from the venue.
- Talk about the math skills that help people figure out what transportation will cost and how long it will take: adding, multiplying, and time.
- Read aloud the real-life scenario above.

Step 2: Overview

- Hand out copies of page 20.
- Review the meanings of *one way* and *round trip*.
- Have students identify the adults (Tyler and Bob), the child (Molly) and the teenagers (Mia and Matt).
- Talk about planning for time. Write on the board the time students need to arrive at school. Then call on students to tell how long it takes them to travel to school. Write the time subtraction problem on the board, for example:

$$\begin{array}{r} 8{:}30 \\ -\ 25 \\ \hline \end{array}$$

- By what time must this student leave home to arrive at school on time? (*8:05*)

Step 3: Guided Questions

Read the transportation chart with students and ask questions to check for understanding:

❶ How many ways to travel did Mia find? (*four*)

❷ Which one is cheapest? (*subway*)

❸ Which is the most expensive? (*ferry*)

❹ Which means of transportation is fastest? (*train*)

❺ Which means of transportation is slowest? (*ferry*)

❻ If it takes 35 minutes to ride the express bus to the stadium and the families want to be at the stadium by 3:05, by what time do the families need to catch the bus? (*2:30 P.M.*)

Let's Work Together

Work through the problems on the page.

Now It's Your Turn

Hand out copies of page 21 and have students work individually or in pairs to complete the *Now It's Your Turn* activity

✳ For answers to reproducibles, see page 63.

Challenge

Mixing It Up

How much will it cost Tyler, Bob, Molly, Mia and Matt to take the subway to the game and the express bus home?

Name _____ Date _____

Go, Team!

TYLER	BOB	MOLLY	MIA	MATT
AGE 45	AGE 42	AGE 9	AGE 13	AGE 15

💡 **Remember!**
Fares are one way.

TRANSPORTATION	FARE	TRAVEL TIME
SUBWAY	$2.50 ADULT OR CHILD (CHILD = UNDER 12)	25 MINUTES
EXPRESS BUS	$5.50 ADULT OR CHILD	35 MINUTES
TRAIN	$5.25 ADULT, $2.75 CHILD	15 MINUTES
FERRY	$12.50 ADULT, $9 CHILD	90 MINUTES

Option 1: Tyler, Bob, Molly, Mia and Matt will go by subway.

How much will the subway cost each way for the whole family? _____

How much will the subway cost round trip?
_____

By what time must they be on the subway if they want to be at the stadium by 3:05 P.M.?
_____

Option 2: The subway is fast, but the express bus is a nicer ride.

How much will the express bus cost each way for the family? _____

How much will the express bus cost round trip?
_____

What time must they be on the bus to get to get to the stadium by 3:05 P.M.?
_____

Option 3: It might be easier to meet in the train station and go from there.

How much will the train cost each way for the family? _____

How much will the train cost round trip?
_____

By what time must they be on the train to get to the stadium by 3:05 P.M.?
_____

Option 4: If the weather is really nice, they could take the ferry for a special treat.

How much will the ferry cost one way for the family? _____

How much will the ferry cost round trip?
_____

By what time must they be on the ferry to get to the stadium by 3:05 P.M.?
_____

Building Real-Life Math Skills • © 2011 by Liane B. Onish • Scholastic Teaching Resources

Name _____ Date _____

Go, Team!

Step 1
Read the chart below.

The Duncans

	Uncle Steve Age 77	Aunt Mimi Age 75	Dan Age 44	Barbara Age 43	Julie Age 9	Sam Age 14

Transportation	Fare	Travel Time
Subway	$2.50 Adult, $1.25 Child (Under 12) or Senior (55 and older)	25 Minutes
Express Bus	$5.50 Adult, $3.50 Child or Senior	35 Minutes
Train	$5.25 Adult, $3.50 Child or Senior	15 Minutes
Ferry	$12.50 Adult, $9 Child or Senior	90 Minutes

Step 2
Answer these questions.

It's Barbara's birthday! The whole Duncan family is heading to a baseball game. They are thinking about taking the ferry. Remember, Uncle Steve and Aunt Mimi are seniors, and Julie is only 9.

1. How much will the ferry cost one way for the whole family? _____

2. How much will the ferry cost round trip?
_____

3. By what time must they be on the ferry if they want to be at the stadium by 12:15 P.M.?
_____

The express bus stops in the Duncans' neighborhood. It is another travel option.

4. How much will an express bus trip to the game cost the whole family?
_____

5. How much will round-trip bus transportation cost? _____

6. By what time must they be on the bus if they want to get to the stadium by 12:15 P.M.?
_____

Sam suggests that the whole family take the train to the game and the subway home.

7. How much will going to the game by train cost the whole family?
_____

8. By what time must they be on the train to get to the stadium by 12:15 P.M.?
_____

9. How much will the subway ride home cost the family? _____

10. If they catch the 4:45 P.M. subway home, what time will they get home?
_____

Building Real-Life Math Skills • © 2011 by Liane B. Onish • Scholastic Teaching Resources

Concert Shop

FOCUS SKILLS:
- Money
- Adding Decimals
- Subtracting Decimals
- Estimating

GET STUFF!

Short-Sleeve T-shirt $18

Long-Sleeve T-shirt $23

Band Hoodie $44.95

Concert CD $12.79

Keychain $4

Water Bottle $11.59

Real-Life Scenario

"The concert is awesome!" said Olivia and Zoe at the same time.

"You guys do that an awful lot," noted Zoe's big brother, Zane.

"That's because we're best friends, Silly," Zoe told him.

"Pick out what you want, buy it, and let's get back to our seats. I don't want to miss anything," Zane replied.

"What should I get?" asked Olivia. "I have $20 to spend."

"I want one of everything," Zoe giggled, "but I only have $25."

"Just make up your minds already," said Zane.

What's at Stake

Figuring out which concert souvenirs you can afford.

Teach

Step 1: Set the Stage

- Ask students to talk about a concert, game, or show they have been to. Invite them to recall souvenirs available for purchase.
- Read aloud the real-life scenario above.

Step 2: Overview

- Hand out copies of page 23.
- Review subtraction with regrouping if needed.
- Review estimating and rounding up. Explain that when we estimate prices, we round the price up to the next higher dollar if the cents are 50¢ or more. We round down to the next lower dollar amount if the cents are less than 50¢.

Step 3: Guided Questions

Guide students to study the items available at the souvenir stand, then ask questions to check for understanding. Explain that in this activity, all prices include sales tax.

❶ How many of the souvenirs cost less than the $20 Olivia has to spend? (*four*)

❷ Which souvenir can neither Olivia nor Zoe (who has $25) buy? (*band hoodie*)

❸ Which souvenir could the girls each buy four of? (*keychain*)

❹ Which souvenir could Zoe afford to buy that Olivia could not? (*long-sleeve T-shirt*)

Let's Work Together

- Before working through the problems on the page, have students practice estimating and subtracting. For example, round up the price of the CD ($13). Estimate the change from $15. Then find the exact change.

  Round up the price of the hoodie ($45). Estimate the change from $50.

  Find the exact change.

- Now work through the problems on the page.

Now It's Your Turn

Distribute copies of page 24 and have students work individually or in pairs to complete the *Now It's Your Turn* activity.

✳ For answers to reproducibles, see page 63.

Challenge

Sales Tax

Explain that in real life, we sometimes need to add sales tax to a price. Have students choose one souvenir and calculate the cost with 4.75% sales tax. If you live in a state with sales tax, calculate the item's cost at your own state rate.

Name _____ Date _____

Concert Shop

GET STUFF!

Short-Sleeve T-shirt $18

Long-Sleeve T-shirt $23

Band Hoodie $44.95

Concert CD $12.79

Keychain $4

Water Bottle $11.59

Key Math Terms

estimate: round to the nearest dollar

change: the money you get back after subtracting purchases from the amount of money you pay

dozen: 12 of something

1. What is the estimated cost of two water bottles?

_____

2. What is the exact cost of two water bottles?

_____

3. What is the estimated cost of two CDs?

_____

4. Olivia buys one item. Her change from $20 is $2. What did she buy?

_____

5. If Zoe could buy one of everything, how much would she spend?

_____

6. Zane's parents asked him to buy a dozen key chains for gifts. How much will Zane spend?

_____

7. When the girls head back to their seats, Zane buys a surprise birthday present for his sister—a band hoodie. How much will he spend on the key chains and hoodie?

_____

8. How much change will Zane get from $100?

_____

Name _____ Date _____

Concert Shop

Step 1
Look at the items for sale at this souvenir stand.

Step 2
Answer these questions.

1. What is the estimated cost of two baseball caps? _____

2. What is the estimated cost of three CDs? _____

3. What is the exact cost of three CDs? _____

4. Daniel has $20 to spend. His change is 6¢. What two items did he buy? _____

5. About how much money does Antonio need to buy three pennants? _____

6. Exactly how much will three pennants cost? _____

7. About how much will Satomi spend on a bandana and pin? Estimate! _____

8. About how much will one of everything cost? Estimate! _____

Spring Carnival

Real-Life Scenario

Theresa and her best friend, Camille, are looking forward to the Rockville Elementary School carnival. Each spring, the school has the carnival to raise money for after-school clubs. This year, the money is going to the woodworking club for new tools.

"Dunk-a-Ball is the best!" said Theresa. "Last year I won a wristwatch!"

"What will you try to win this year?" asked Camille.

"I'm going to aim for that giant panda," said Theresa, pointing to the display of prizes. "I have $10. I hope that will be enough. What about you?"

Camille said, "I have $12. I want to play Ring-the-Bats. I hope I can win a great birthday present for my brother."

What's at Stake
Determining how many points you need to win the prizes you want.

Teach

Step 1: Set the Stage
- Invite students to describe carnivals, arcades, and/or street fairs they have been to and the games they've played there. Ask them to recall how much each game cost, the rules of the game, and how prizes were awarded.
- Read aloud the real-life scenario above.

Step 2: Overview
- Hand out copies of page 26 and look at the game sign with students.
- Review addition and subtraction if necessary.
- Ask students to tell what operation they would use to figure out how many points a player has won if she tossed the first ball into the large basket, the second ball into the medium basket, and the third ball into the small basket. (*addition*) Ask: How many points did the player win? (*1 + 5 + 10 = 16*)
- Ask: If the player wanted to win a wristwatch, what operation would you use to figure out how many more points she needed? (*subtraction*) How many more points would she need? (*25 – 16 = 9*)
- Review division and multiplication if necessary.
- Ask: If a player has $8, how many times can he play Dunk-a-Ball? (*four*) What operation did you use to find the answer? (*division*)

- Ask: If that player plays four times, how many balls will he get to throw? (*12*) What operation did you use? (*multiplication: 4 games x 3 balls per game*)

Step 3: Guided Questions
Ask questions to check for understanding:

❶ How much does each game of Dunk-a-Ball cost? (*$2*)

❷ How many balls do you get to throw in each game? (*three*)

❸ How many points do you win for throwing a ball into the medium basket? (*five*)

❹ If you threw a ball into the large basket every time, how many games would you have to play to win 12 points? Remember: You get three balls in each game. (*four*)

Let's Work Together
Work through the problems on the page.

Now It's Your Turn
Distribute copies of page 27 and have students work individually or in pairs to complete the Now It's Your Turn activity.

✳ For answers to reproducibles, see page 63.

Name _____ Date _____

Spring Carnival

1. Theresa spent $6 at the Dunk-a-Ball game. How many times did she play?

   _____

2. How many balls did she throw?

   _____

3. How much did each ball cost? Round up to the nearest hundredth, or penny.

   _____

4. In her first game, Theresa got only two balls in the baskets. She scored six points. Which baskets did she toss the balls into?

   _____

5. In her second game, Theresa got three balls in the baskets. She scored 11 points. Which baskets did she toss the balls into?

   _____

6. In her third game, Theresa got two balls in the baskets. She scored 20 points. Which baskets did she toss the balls into?

   _____

7. How many points did Theresa win in all?

   _____

8. What two prizes could Theresa get that would use all of her points?

   _____

9. If Theresa started with $10 and played three games, how much money does she have left?

   _____

10. How much would it cost to throw 24 balls at this game?

   _____

Building Real-Life Math Skills • © 2011 by Liane B. Onish • Scholastic Teaching Resources

Name _____ Date _____

Spring Carnival

Step 1

Read the sign for the carnival game.

RING-THE-BATS 4 RINGS FOR $3

Get Your Ring Around A Bat!

Striped Bat = 2 Points
Polka Dot Bat = 3 Points
Star Bat = 4 Points
Checkerboard Bat = 5 Points

Prizes
15 points = Inflatable Alien
12 points = Bag of Marbles
10 points = Paddle Ball
8 points = Insect Finger Puppets

Step 2

Answer these questions.

1. Camille played three games of Ring-the-Bats. How much did she spend?

_____

2. How many rings did Camille throw?

_____

3. How much did each ring cost?

_____

4. In her first game, Camille got rings around two bats. She scored five points. Which bats did she get?

_____

5. In her second game, Camille got rings around three different bats. She scored 10 points. Which bats did she ring?

_____

6. In her third game, Camille got rings around four different bats. How many points did she score?

_____

7. How many points did Camille win in all?

_____

8. If Camille gets an inflatable alien for her brother, how many points will she have left?

_____

9. Together, Camille and her friend Theresa have 21 leftover points. The girls want to get two prizes to share. What two prizes could they get? List all of their options.

_____

_____

Making Money

Real-Life Scenario

Amy's big sister, Candace, babysits. Candace puts half of the money she earns into a savings account. She spends the rest on clothes and going out with friends. Amy is only nine years old. She is too young to babysit, but she wants to make money, too.

Candace helps Amy make a list of things she could do to earn money. Then they make a flier to put up around town.

The very next day, Amy gets her first job! Mrs. Applegate across the street wants Amy to water her house plants. Now Amy goes to Mrs. Applegate's house on Monday, Wednesday, and Friday. And Candace got a new babysitting job, too!

Remember
Some jobs pay by the hour or half hour. Other jobs pay by the day.

What's at Stake
Earning spending money.

Teach

Step 1: Set the Stage
- Ask students to name chores or jobs they do to earn their allowance or extra cash. List these jobs on the board. Talk about what students spend their money on. Do they regularly put money aside to save? Are they saving for a big purchase or saving for the future?
- Talk about the math skills that will help students figure out how much they earn and save: addition, subtraction, multiplication, and time.
- Read aloud the real-life scenario above.

Step 2: Overview
- Hand out copies of page 30.
- Review fractions and decimals. Write these fractions on the board and ask students to name the decimal equivalents:

$$\frac{1}{4} = 0.25 \qquad \frac{1}{2} = 0.50 \qquad \frac{3}{4} = 0.75$$

- Review time.

$$30 \text{ minutes} = \frac{1}{2} \text{ hour}$$

$$15 \text{ minutes} = \frac{1}{4} \text{ hour}$$

$$45 \text{ minutes} = \frac{3}{4} \text{ hour}$$

$$60 \text{ minutes} = 1 \text{ hour}$$

$$7 \text{ days} = 1 \text{ week}$$

$$52 \text{ weeks} = 1 \text{ year}$$

- Explain that if a worker is paid by the hour, students can find total wages by multiplying the hourly rate of pay by the number of hours worked. If a worker works only part of an hour, students must multiply the hourly rate of pay by the fraction or decimal that represents that part of an hour.

- To demonstrate, review multiplication of fractions. Remind students to give any whole numbers a denominator of 1 and to multiply the numerators and the denominators straight across. Have them practice using the problems below, stating the answers in lowest terms:

$$\frac{1}{2} \times \frac{15}{1} = \frac{15}{2} \text{ or } 7\frac{1}{2}$$

$$\frac{3}{4} \times \frac{20}{1} = \frac{60}{4} \text{ or } 15$$

Teach continued

• Point out that if students prefer, they can convert fractions into decimals before multiplying. Review multiplication of decimals, reminding students that they do not need to align the decimals. Instead, they should multiply as if working with whole numbers. Then, when they have completed the problem, they should count the number of decimal places to the right of the decimals in the problem, then insert the decimal in the answer by starting at the right and counting over that number of places. Demonstrate with the following example. Notice that it is the same problem that appears above:

```
   .75  ← count 2 places after the decimal
 x  20  ← count 0 places after the decimal
 ─────
   00
 1500
 ─────
 15.00 ← Total decimal places above was 2, so
          count 2 decimal places from the right
          and insert decimal.
```

Answer = 15.00 or 15

Step 3: Guided Questions
Read the flier with students and ask questions to check for understanding:

❶ Amy helps Mrs. Applegate water her plants three days a week. How much does Amy earn in a week? (*$15*) How much does she earn in two weeks? (*$30*)

❷ Would Amy earn more by working in a neighbor's garden for three hours or watching a friend's cat for two days? (*$4 more by working in the garden*)

❸ Candace babysits three hours on Saturday and two hours on Sunday. How much does she earn over the weekend? (*$60*) What are two ways to solve the problem? (*You can multiply $12 by 5 hours or calculate each day's earnings separately and then add.*)

❹ If Candace saves half of her weekend's earnings, how much does she have left to spend on purchases and activities? (*$30*)

Let's Work Together
Work through the problems on the page.

Now It's Your Turn
Distribute copies of page 31 and have students work individually or in pairs to complete the *Now It's Your Turn* activity.

✳ For answers to reproducibles, see page 63.

Challenge

Bonus
Pick a chore or activity you could do from Amy's list. Figure out how much you would earn if you worked twice a week for one year. Now imagine that your parents agree to give you a 10% bonus on the total amount. How much is your bonus?

Name _____ Date _____

Making Money

I can:

Walk your dog:
$15 Per 30 minutes

Take care of your cat:
$10 Per day

Water your plants:
$5 Per day

Help in the garden:
$8 Per hour

Candace can:
Babysit your children: $12 Per hour

My name is Amy, and I am 9 years old.

My big sister Candace is 17 years old.

Remember!
Some jobs pay by the hour or half hour. Other jobs pay by the day.

1. In the winter, Mrs. Applegate's house is very dry. She asks Amy to help water her plants every day (including weekends). How much will Amy earn in a week?

   _____

2. If Amy waters Mrs. Applegate's plants every day for 10 weeks, how much will she earn?

   _____

3. Amy is saving up for a new bike. After 10 weeks of watering Mrs. Applegate's plants every day, she puts half of her earnings in the bank. How much does she have left?

   _____

4. Amy's other neighbors, the Olivers, are going away for one weekend. They need Amy to take care of their cat on Saturday and Sunday. How much will Amy earn cat sitting?

   _____

5. In the spring, the Olivers ask Amy to help in their garden $3\frac{1}{2}$ hours each week. How much does Amy earn in a week?

   _____

6. If Amy helps in the Olivers' garden for 12 weeks, how much will she earn?

   _____

7. Amy's sister, Candace, babysits an average of $6\frac{3}{4}$ hours a week. About how much does she earn in four weeks?

   _____

8. If Candace continues babysitting $6\frac{3}{4}$ hours each week for an entire year, about how much will she earn? Remember: A year has 52 weeks.

   _____

Building Real-Life Math Skills • © 2011 by Liane B. Onish • Scholastic Teaching Resources

Name _____   Date _____

Making Money

Step 1

Jamal and James want to earn some money. Read their flier to see what they can do.

Step 2

Answer these questions.

1. James and Jamal are favorite neighborhood dog walkers. James walks a neighbor's Irish setter for half an hour each day Monday through Friday. How much does James earn in a week?

_____

2. Jamal walks another neighbor's poodle and cocker spaniel for half an hour each day Monday through Friday. How much does Jamal earn walking the two dogs?

_____

3. One weekend, James walks the Irish setter for an hour on Saturday and an hour on Sunday. How much does he earn that weekend?

_____

4. In the fall, the twins help rake leaves. During the month of October, James raked for $11\frac{1}{2}$ hours. How much did he earn?

_____

5. Jamal also raked leaves in October. He worked nine hours. How much did Jamal earn?

_____

6. How much more time did James spend raking in October than Jamal? How much more did he earn?

_____

7. The year's first big snowstorm was on Thanksgiving. James shoveled snow for 3 hours that weekend. Jamal shoveled snow for $2\frac{1}{2}$ hours. How much did the twins earn shoveling snow in all?

_____

8. Would James earn more money walking two dogs for two hours or shoveling snow for six hours?

At the Supermarket

Real-Life Scenario

"I think that's everything on the list," Adrienne said.

Mom opened her overstuffed handbag. She said, "Honey, please figure out about how much all of this will cost while I hunt for my wallet."

Adrienne said, "But Mom! My calculator is at home."

Mom said, "Estimate—you know, round up or down and then add. I know you can do that without a calculator."

What's at Stake

Estimating the cost of groceries to make sure you have enough cash.

1 Jar of Tomato Sauce
Price: $3.69 a Jar

Head of Lettuce
Price: $1.79 Each

1 Bag of Carrots
Price: 2 Bags for $1.50

1.5 Pounds of Ground Beef
Price: $2.69 per Pound

Pint of Raspberries
Price: $1.75 Each

Container of Ice Cream
Price: $2.89 Each

1 Cucumber
Price: 4 for $2.00

Quart of Milk
Price: $1.19 Each

1 Box of Spaghetti
Price: 5 Boxes for $4.00

1 Bottle of Salad Dressing
Price: $2.55 Each

Pint of Grape Tomatoes
Price: $2.39 Each

Teach

Step 1: Set the Stage

- Ask students to name some of their favorite family meals eaten at home. Encourage them to talk about times when they have helped with the shopping.
- Talk about the main math skills that help them figure out shopping costs: estimate, round up, round down, addition, and division.
- Read aloud the real-life scenario above.

Step 2: Overview

- Hand out copies of page 34.
- Review estimating and rounding up. Explain that when we estimate prices, such as food items at the market, we round up the price to the next higher dollar if the cents are 50¢ or greater. Write $1.79 on the board. Have students round up. Write $2.00 next to it. Repeat for $3.59 ($4.00) and $2.95 ($3.00).

$1.79	$2.00
$3.59	$4.00
$2.95	$3.00

- Review rounding down. Explain that when the cents are less than 50¢, we round down to the next lowest dollar amount. For example: $1.39 rounds down to $1.00, $6.49 rounds down to $6.00. Add the following amounts to the list on the board and have students round down:

$3.25	$3.00
$1.19	$1.00
$6.39	$6.00

- Review estimating a total. Explain that to estimate a total, we can round up or down and then add the rounded numbers together. Discuss that adding estimated numbers is math students can do in their heads, whereas adding a column of figures is difficult to do as mental math. Have one student volunteer estimate the total of the six money amounts described above ($1.79, $3.59, $2.95, $3.25, $1.19, and $6.39) while another volunteer calculates the exact total. Together, find the difference between the estimate ($19) and the exact amount ($19.35).

- Point out that sometimes items in a store are priced together (several items for a certain price) and students may need to calculate the price for one. Review division with decimals. Write (or draw) on the board: "two apples for $1.00." Ask students to name the operation they will use to find out how much one apple costs (division). Have a volunteer draw a picture or use your illustration to calculate the answer (50¢). Repeat, if needed, with two cartons of juice for $5.00 ($2.50).

Teach continued

Step 3: Guided Questions

Take a look at the items in the shopping cart with students. Then ask questions to check for understanding:

❶ Which item in the cart is priced by the pound? (*ground beef*)

❷ Which items in the cart are group priced, meaning that the price is given for multiple units and the shopper has to figure out the price for one unit? (*boxes of spaghetti, cucumbers, and bags of carrots*)

❸ Adrienne's mom bought one box of spaghetti. How much did she spend on spaghetti? What operation did you use? (*80¢; division*)

❹ Round up or down the cost of tomato sauce. (*round up to $4*)

❺ Estimate the cost of the spaghetti and the sauce together. (*$5*)

❻ What is the actual cost of the spaghetti and the sauce? (*$4.49*)

❼ What operation can you use to find the difference between the estimate and the actual cost? (*subtraction*)

❽ What is the difference between the estimate and the actual cost? (*51¢*)

Let's Work Together

Now work through the problems on the page. Remind students to look carefully at the quantity of each item in the cart before they estimate or calculate prices.

Now It's Your Turn

Distribute copies of page 35 and have students work individually or in pairs to complete the *Now It's Your Turn* activity.

✳ For answers to reproducibles, see page 63.

Challenge

Making Meatballs

Look again at the shopping cart on page 34. Imagine that Adrienne's mom is planning to make meatballs this week. She has placed 1.5 pounds of ground beef in her cart, which is enough to make nine meatballs. How many meatballs can she make with one pound of ground beef?

Key Math Terms

estimate: to make a rough calculation

round up: to change a number to the next higher amount (in this case, the next whole dollar amount). For example: Round $1.86 up to $2.00; round $2.57 up to $3.00; round $3.77 up to $4.00.

round down: to change a number to the nearest lower amount (in this case, the next lower whole dollar amount). For example: Round $1.14 down to $1.00; round $2.42 down to $2.00; round $3.35 down to $3.00.

Name _____ Date _____

At the Supermarket

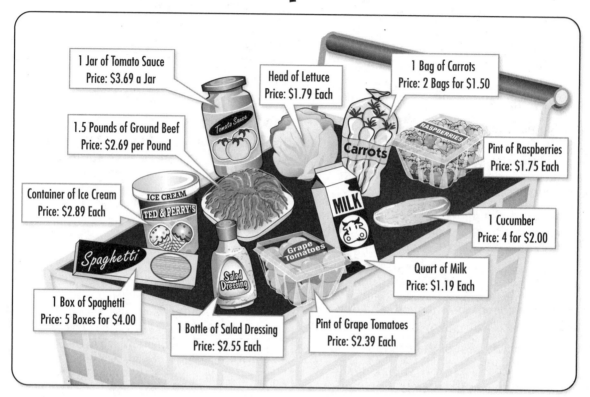

1. Adrienne's mom bought one bag of carrots. How much is one bag? _____
   What operation did you use?

   _____

2. Now estimate the cost of the bag of carrots to the nearest dollar. Did you round up or down?

   _____

3. Adrienne's mom bought one cucumber. How much is one cucumber? _____

4. Estimate the cost of the cucumber to the nearest dollar. _____

5. What is the estimated cost of one bottle of salad dressing? _____

6. What is the estimated cost of the lettuce?

   _____

7. What is the estimated cost of the tomatoes?

   _____

8. The lettuce, tomatoes, carrots, cucumber, and dressing are for a salad. What is the estimated cost of all the salad ingredients?

   _____

9. What is the actual cost of the salad ingredients? _____

10. What is the estimated cost of all the items in the shopping cart?

    _____

 Remember! Round the price up to the next higher dollar if the cents are 50¢ or more. Round down to the next lower dollar if the cents are less than 50¢. To estimate the cost, add the rounded amounts together.

Building Real-Life Math Skills • © 2011 by Liane B. Onish • Scholastic Teaching Resources

Name _____   Date _____

At the Supermarket

Step 1

Look at the items in Ethan's shopping basket.

1 Bottle Barbecue Sauce
Price: $2.59 Each

2 Pounds Chicken Legs
Price: $1.19 a Pound

1 Bag Baking Potatoes
Price: $3.79 a Bag

1 Pound Cherries
Price: $3.88 a Pound

BB-Q Sauce

2 Pound Package CHICKEN LEGS

5 Pound Bag Baking POTATOES

Cherries

FROZEN MIXED VEGETABLES

1 Box Frozen Vegetables
Price: 3 Boxes for $6

Step 2

Answer these questions.

1. Diego's dad bought one box of frozen mixed vegetables. What operation will you use to find the cost of one box?

_____

How much is one box? _____

2. Round the cost of the bag of potatoes to the nearest dollar. Did you round up or down?

_____

3. What is the estimated cost of the chicken legs in the cart? _____

4. What is the estimated cost of the barbecue sauce?

_____

5. What is the estimated cost of the pound of cherries? _____

6. What is the estimated total cost of all the items in the basket?

_____

7. What is the actual cost of all the items in the basket?

_____

8. Diego's dad paid for the food with a $20 bill. How much change did he get?

_____

9. Diego's dad gives the change to Diego to buy some cupcakes. If cupcakes cost $1.79 each, how many cupcakes can Diego buy?

Pizza! Pizza!

FOCUS SKILLS:
- Fractions
- Money

Real-Life Scenario

Matt's mom knew the answer, but asked the question anyway. "What do you want to eat at your birthday party, Matt?"

"Pizza!" exclaimed the 9-going-on-10-year-old.

"And salad," his dad added.

Matt counted the friends and family who would be at his celebration. He announced that 14 people would be eating the pizza.

"And salad," his dad added.

"How many pizzas do we need?" Matt asked.

"You're the big birthday boy. We'll give you the menu and let you figure it out," said his mom.

Dad began to say, "And don't forget..."

"I know. Salad!" said Matt, finishing the sentence.

What's at Stake

Figuring out how much pizza and salad to order for a group—and how much it will cost.

Teach

Step 1: Set the Stage

- Ask students to raise their hands if they like pizza. Talk about how often they eat pizza and what toppings they like best.
- Talk about the math skills that will help them figure out how much the pizza and salad will cost: fractions as well as addition, subtraction, and division with money.
- Read aloud the real-life scenario above.

Step 2: Overview

- Hand out copies of page 38.
- Review fractional parts of a whole. Have volunteers draw circles on the board. Have other students divide the circles into different fractional pieces: halves, quarters, thirds, sixths, and eighths. Ask other students to shade in fractional amounts, such as $\frac{1}{2}$, $\frac{2}{3}$, $\frac{3}{4}$, $\frac{1}{6}$, and $\frac{5}{8}$. Have them write the fraction under the shaded circles. For additional review, repeat with squares or rectangles.
- Review the parts of a fraction:

$$\frac{1}{4}$$
1 ← **numerator**
4 ← **denominator**

- Review equivalent fractions. Have students illustrate $\frac{2}{8}$ by drawing a circle and dividing it into eight sections and shading $\frac{2}{8}$. Then have them draw a second circle and divide it into four sections and shade $\frac{1}{4}$. How many eighths in $\frac{1}{4}$? Repeat for $\frac{2}{4}$, $\frac{3}{4}$, and $\frac{4}{4}$.
- Review renaming fractions in lowest terms. Remind students that to find the lowest terms, divide the numerator and denominator by common factors until there is no common factor left that is greater than 1. For example:

$$\frac{2}{8} \div \frac{2}{2} = \frac{1}{4}$$

Repeat with these fractions: $\frac{3}{6}$, $\frac{8}{10}$, $\frac{12}{16}$

$$\frac{3}{6} \div \frac{3}{3} = \frac{1}{2} \qquad \frac{8}{10} \div \frac{2}{2} = \frac{4}{5} \qquad \frac{12}{16} \div \frac{4}{4} = \frac{3}{4}$$

- Have students illustrate finding common denominators by dividing the quarters of the second circle in half, forming eighths, and comparing it to the first circle.
- Review working with money, reminding students to line up the decimal points when adding or subtracting.

Teach   continued

- Demonstrate how to divide with decimals, encouraging students to round answers to the nearest hundredth. For younger students, consider having them use calculators for this portion of the lesson. Use the following as an example: If one pizza pie costs $12.50 and has six slices, about how much does each slice cost?

$$
\begin{array}{r}
2.08333\overline{}\ (\text{or } 2.08) \\
6\,\overline{)\,12.50} \\
-12 \\
\hline
0 \\
50 \\
-48 \\
\hline
2
\end{array}
$$

Step 3: Guided Questions

Read the pizza menu with students and ask questions to check for understanding:

❶ How many slices are in a small pizza from this pizza parlor? (*four slices*) A medium pizza? (*six slices*) A large pizza? (*eight slices*)

❷ How many slices are in ½ of a medium pizza? (*three slices*)

❸ How many slices are in ¼ of a large pizza? (*two slices*)

❹ How much will one small, one medium and one large plain cheese pie cost in all? (*$34.50*) What is the approximate cost of each slice? Hint: round up to the nearest dollar. (*about $2*)

❺ If you buy a small pie and eat three slices, what fraction of the pie is left? (¼)

❻ If you buy a large pie and eat five slices, what fraction of the pie is left? (⅜)

❼ If you buy a medium pie and eat three slices, what fraction of the pie is left? Name the fraction in lowest terms. (³⁄₆, *or* ½)

❽ How many salad servings would you get if you bought three party-size salads? (*24*)

Let's Work Together
Work through the problems on the page.

Now It's Your Turn
Distribute copies of page 39 and have students work individually or in pairs to complete the *Now It's Your Turn* activity.

✳ For answers to reproducibles, see page 64.

Challenge

Pizza for a Crowd

Look again at the menu on page 38. If you need 50 slices of pizza, what are your options for ordering? How much does each option cost?

Name _____ Date _____

Pizza! Pizza!

PIZZA & SALAD MENU

Small (4 Slices)
Cheese Pie $7.50
With 1 Extra Topping $8.95

Medium (6 Slices)
Cheese Pie $11.50
With 1 Extra Topping $13.50

Large (8 Slices)
Cheese Pie $15.50
With 1 Extra Topping $17.50

Small
House Salad $4.25
Serves 2

Medium
House Salad $8.25
Serves 4

Party-Size
House Salad $15.95
Serves 8

Placing the Order

1. For Matt's party, his family orders one medium pepperoni pizza, two large cheese pizzas, and one large pizza with mushrooms. How many slices of pizza do they order in all?

   _____

2. How much will their whole pizza order cost?

   _____

3. About how much will each slice cost in their order?

   _____

4. There will be 14 people at Matt's party. About how many slices can each person eat?

   _____

5. About how much is each serving of a party-size salad? [*Hint: round up the cost of the salad to the nearest dollar and then divide by 8.*]

   _____

6. Matt's family wants to order exactly enough salad for 14 servings. What is the least expensive way to order the salad?

   _____

Leftovers!

It turns out that the party guests were not as hungry as Matt's family expected. There are seven slices of pizza left.

7. One slice of the medium pepperoni pizza is left. What fraction of that pie is left?

   _____

8. Only two slices of the large mushroom pizza were eaten. What fraction of the pie is left? Name the fraction in lowest terms.

   _____

9. What fraction of the total number of ordered pizza slices did the party guests eat?

Building Real-Life Math Skills • © 2011 by Liane B. Onish • Scholastic Teaching Resources

Name _____ Date _____

Pizza! Pizza!

Step 1

Madeleine's soccer team loves Yummy Pizza Parlor. Read the menu to see what the restaurant has to offer.

Step 2

Answer these questions.

1. After practice, 10 soccer players and their two coaches go to Yummy Pizza Parlor for pizza. If each player wants one slice and each coach wants two slices, how many slices do they need in all?

   _____

2. Name three different ways the team could order exactly the number of slices they need. How much does each option cost?

   Option 1: _____

   _____

   Option 2: _____

   _____

   Option 3: _____

   _____

3. The team decides to order two large pies in case any of the kids decides to eat a second slice. How much will the two pies cost?

   _____

4. In the end, the group eats 15 slices. What fraction of a large pie is left over?

   _____

5. If each coach eats two slices, what fraction of a large pie do the coaches eat? _____

6. If each coach eats two slices, what fraction of the total amount of ordered pizza do the coaches eat? _____

7. Four team members want salad with their pizza. The coaches find the cheapest way to buy four servings of salad. How do they order the salad? _____

8. For two large pies and four salad servings, what does the team spend? _____

Building Real-Life Math Skills • © 2011 by Liane B. Onish • Scholastic Teaching Resources

Playland

FOCUS SKILL:
○ Converting units of measurement

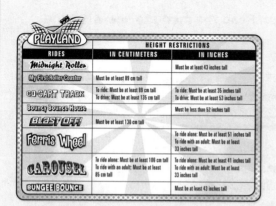

RIDES	HEIGHT RESTRICTIONS	
	IN CENTIMETERS	IN INCHES
Midnight Roller		Must be at least 43 inches tall
My First Roller Coaster	Must be at least 89 cm tall	
GO-CART TRACK	To ride: Must be at least 89 cm tall / To drive: Must be at least 135 cm tall	To ride: Must be at least 35 inches tall / To drive: Must be at least 53 inches tall
Bouncy Bounce House		Must be less than 52 inches tall
BLAST OFF!	Must be at least 130 cm tall	
Ferris Wheel		To ride alone: Must be at least 51 inches tall / To ride with an adult: Must be at least 33 inches tall
CAROUSEL	To ride alone: Must be at least 106 cm tall / To ride with an adult: Must be at least 85 cm tall	To ride alone: Must be at least 41 inches tall / To ride with an adult: Must be at least 33 inches tall
BUNGEE BOUNCE		Must be at least 43 inches tall

Real-Life Scenario

Paula and her 5-year-old sister, Penny, were excited. Their cousin, Pierre, was visiting from France, and Paula's mom had agreed to take all three kids to Playland Amusement Park.

"I can't wait to show you the cool rides we have!" Paula told her cousin.

Paula's mother pointed to a sign at the entrance to the amusement park. "Look, Paula and Pierre. There are the height requirements. Figure out which rides you can go on."

"Me, too!" cried Penny.

"Don't worry, little Penny," said Pierre. "We will find fun for you, too."

As the kids approached the sign, they saw a big problem. The sign was not yet finished. Some of the height requirements were given only in centimeters. Others were given only in inches. It looked like it would be up to them to do some math!

What's at Stake
Determining whether you are tall enough to go on rides.

Teach

Step 1: Set the Stage
• Ask students to tell how tall they are. Or, measure the heights of student volunteers using a yardstick, ruler, or tape measure. Write the heights in feet and inches on the board. Remind students that " is the symbol for inches and ' is the symbol for feet. Talk about times they have been pleased to discover that they were tall enough to go on rides, or disappointed to learn that they were too small.

• Point out that in many countries, people measure height in meters and centimeters (the metric system). In the U.S., we measure height in feet and inches (U.S. standard measurements). To accommodate visitors, some amusement parks give their ride height requirements in both metric and standard forms. Others give requirements in one form (either centimeters or inches) and expect visitors to convert the measurements if needed.

• Talk about the math skills that might help students determine if they meet the height restrictions for amusement park rides anywhere in the world: converting height in feet and inches into height in inches, converting meters or centimeters to inches, converting inches to centimeters.

• Read aloud the real-life scenario above.

Step 2: Overview
• Hand out copies of page 42.

• Review U.S. standard length measures (inches and feet). Remind students how to convert inches to feet and feet to inches. Have students work in pairs to measure each other's height. Have them record the number in feet and inches and then in inches only.

• Give students random heights to convert to inches, for example: 5' 6" (*66 inches*), 4' 2" (*50 inches*), and 3' 7" (*43 inches*). Talk about the operations students used to convert

Teach continued

their height in feet and inches to inches (*multiply feet by 12 inches; add additional inches*).

- Have students try the reverse process—converting inches into feet and inches. Invite them to express the following heights in feet and inches: 68" (*5' 8"*), 55" (*4' 7"*), and 49" (*4' 1"*).

- Now introduce metric measurements. Distribute rulers with inches and centimeters for students to examine. Have them note that an inch is about 2½ centimeters, and a foot is a little more than 30 centimeters.

- Review the formula for converting inches to centimeters (inches x 2.54 centimeters). Be sure students make the connection between 2.54 centimeters and the estimate of 2½ centimeters to an inch they had made by looking at the ruler. Have students convert their own heights into centimeters and round up the numbers to the nearest one. They can then do the same for the practice heights introduced earlier (66, 50, and 43 inches) (*66" = 168 cm, 50" = 127 cm, 43" = 109 cm*).

- Review the formula for converting centimeters to inches (cm x .39 inches). Explain to students that .39 is rounded down from 0.3937008. Have students convert these centimeters to inches: 150 cm (*58.5" or 59"*), 87 cm (*33.9" or 34"*), and 120 cm (*46.8" or 47"*).

Step 3: Guided Questions

Review the sign with ride height requirements with students. Then ask questions to check for understanding:

❶ How many rides have height minimums? (*seven*)

❷ What is a height maximum? (*You can't be taller than a certain height to ride the ride*) Which ride has a height maximum? (*Bouncy Bounce House*)

❸ On the unfinished sign, how many rides list their height restrictions only in centimeters? (*two*)

❹ How many rides list their height restrictions only in inches? (*four*)

❺ Which rides list their height restrictions in both units? (*Go-Cart Track and Carousel*)

❻ How can we find the height in inches if we know the height in centimeters? (*multiply by 0.39 and round up or down*)

❼ How can we find the height in centimeters when we know the height in inches? (*multiply by 2.54 and round up or down*)

❽ If a child is 4' 3" tall, how many inches tall is he? (*multiply 4' x 12 = 48, then add 3 more inches = 51*)

❾ How many centimeters tall is that child? (*Multiply 51 x 2.54 = 129.54; round up to 130 cm*)

❿ According to the sign, would that child be allowed to ride the Go Carts? (*yes*) Would he be allowed to drive? (*no*)

Let's Work Together
Work through the problems on the page.

Now It's Your Turn
Distribute copies of page 43 and have students work individually or in pairs to complete the *Now It's Your Turn* activity.

✷ For answers to reproducibles, see page 64.

Challenge

Family Feet, Inches, and Centimeters
List your family members and their heights. Then calculate how many centimeters tall each person is.

Name _____ Date _____

Playland

RIDES	HEIGHT RESTRICTIONS	
PLAYLAND	**IN CENTIMETERS**	**IN INCHES**
Midnight Roller		Must be at least 43 inches tall
My First Roller Coaster	Must be at least 89 cm tall	
GO-CART TRACK	To ride: Must be at least 89 cm tall To drive: Must be at least 135 cm tall	To ride: Must be at least 35 inches tall To drive: Must be at least 53 inches tall
Bouncy Bounce House		Must be less than 52 inches tall
BLAST OFF!	Must be at least 130 cm tall	
Ferris Wheel		To ride alone: Must be at least 51 inches tall To ride with an adult: Must be at least 33 inches tall
CAROUSEL	To ride alone: Must be at least 106 cm tall To ride with an adult: Must be at least 85 cm tall	To ride alone: Must be at least 41 inches tall To ride with an adult: Must be at least 33 inches tall
BUNGEE BOUNCE		Must be at least 43 inches tall

First, fill in the missing height restrictions on the chart. Round up or down to the nearest whole number.

1. How tall in centimeters must you be to ride the Midnight Roller? _____

2. You must be less than how many centimeters tall to go on the Bouncy Bounce House?

   _____

3. How tall in centimeters must you be to ride the Bungee Bounce? _____

4. How tall in centimeters must you be to ride the Ferris Wheel alone? _____

   With an adult? _____

5. How tall in inches must you be to ride My First Roller Coaster? _____

6. How tall in inches must you be to ride Blast Off? _____

Now, figure out who can go on which rides!

7. Penny is 3' 6" tall. Can she ride My First Roller Coaster? _____

8. Pierre is 140 cm tall. Is he tall enough to ride the Ferris Wheel alone? _____

9. Paula is 4' 10" tall. Can she drive the Go Carts?

   _____

10. What can Penny do that Paula and Pierre cannot? _____

    Why? _____

Remember! To change centimeters to inches: ____ centimeters x 0.39* = in
To change inches to centimeters: ____ inches x 2.54 = cm
***Note:** .39 is a rounding down of 0.3937008

Building Real-Life Math Skills • © 2011 by Liane B. Onish • Scholastic Teaching Resources

Name _____ Date _____

Playland

Step 1

When it gets hot, Paula, Penny, and Pierre head to the water park section of Playland. Read the sign that lists height restrictions for the water park.

WATER RIDES Guests Under 43" (____ cm) Must Wear a Life Vest at All Times	HEIGHT RESTRICTIONS	
	CENTIMETERS	**INCHES**
Monster Squid Water Slide		Must be at least 48" tall to ride
GUPPY ZONE	Must be under 114 cm tall to ride	
LOGS AWAY!		Must be at least 45" tall to ride
REALLY RAPID RAPIDS RIDE		Must be at least 38" tall to ride
Typhoon Tides		Must be under 60" tall to ride
Pirates !	Must be at least 89 cm to ride	Must be at least 35" tall to ride

Step 2

Answer these questions.

Remember to round up or down to the nearest whole number. For questions 1 through 6, add your answers to the blanks on the sign.

1. How tall in centimeters must you be to go on the Monster Squid Water Slide?

   _____

2. How tall in centimeters must you be to ride Logs Away? _____

3. How tall in centimeters must you be to ride the Really Rapid Rapids Ride?

   _____

4. You must be under how many centimeters tall to ride Typhoon Tides? _____

5. You must be under how many inches tall to ride Guppy Zone? _____

6. The sign says that guests under 43" tall must wear a life vest at all times. How many centimeters is that? _____

7. Penny is 3' 6" tall. Pierre is 140 cm tall. Paula is 4' 10" tall. Do any of them need to wear a life vest? _____

8. Is Pierre tall enough to go on the Monster Squid Water Slide? _____

9. What can Penny ride that Paula and Pierre cannot?

   _____

10. How many inches must Penny grow before she can go on the Logs Away ride?

   _____

Muffins Versus Cupcakes

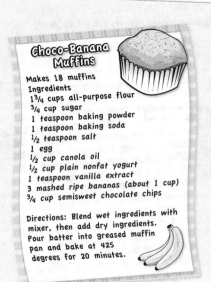

Choco-Banana Muffins

Makes 18 muffins
Ingredients
1¾ cups all-purpose flour
¾ cup sugar
1 teaspoon baking powder
1 teaspoon baking soda
½ teaspoon salt
1 egg
½ cup canola oil
½ cup plain nonfat yogurt
1 teaspoon vanilla extract
3 mashed ripe bananas (about 1 cup)
¾ cup semisweet chocolate chips

Directions: Blend wet ingredients with mixer, then add dry ingredients. Pour batter into greased muffin pan and bake at 425 degrees for 20 minutes.

Real-Life Scenario

A baked-goods battle was raging in the Meyers house. The family had to make treats for an upcoming community bake sale. Daniel wanted to make chocolate cupcakes, but his sister, Kim, argued that muffins would be a tastier and more nutritious choice.

"I think what we need here is less arguing and more baking," interjected their dad. "Why don't you make both muffins and cupcakes? Get your recipes ready, gather the ingredients, and get started! Just remember, we promised to make 72 treats for the bake sale. It looks like you two will be busy for a while!"

What's at Stake
Being able to compare recipes and double a recipe to feed a crowd.

Teach

Step 1: Set the Stage

- Ask students to talk about baking they or family members do at home. Who bakes? What do they bake? What are students' favorite home-baked foods?
- Talk about the math skills that will help students compare and work with recipe amounts: standard measurements and fractions.
- Read aloud the real-life scenario above.

Step 2: Overview

- Hand out copies of page 46.
- Discuss students' opinions on whether there really is a difference between muffins and cupcakes (in terms of nutrition and/or taste).
- Have students preview the ingredients and list on the board the measuring tools they would need for the recipes: measuring spoons (⅛, ¼, ½, 1 teaspoon; tablespoon), measuring cups (¼, ⅓, ½, and 1 cup). Explain that cups, teaspoons, and tablespoons are all examples of U.S. standard measurements.
- Guide students to notice the number of servings each recipe makes (*18*). Remind them

that Kim and Daniel need to make a total of 72 baked goods. Ask: If Kim and Daniel split the baking evenly, how many muffins will Kim bake? How many cupcakes will Daniel bake? What will they need to do to their recipes? (*double them*) Review that doubling a recipe entails multiplying each ingredient by 2 or adding the amount twice.

- Remind students that when working with fractions, they sometimes need to change mixed numbers to improper fractions. Review the process, then write these mixed numbers on the board and have students name the improper fraction for each mixed number: 1½ (³⁄₂); 2¼ (⁹⁄₄).
- Review how to add fractions, finding a common denominator if necessary. For example, if a recipe calls for ¾ cup sugar and you are doubling the recipe, you will need to add:

$$\frac{3}{4} + \frac{3}{4} = \frac{6}{4}$$

In this case, demonstrate how to rename the improper fraction to 1¾ or 1½.

- Demonstrate how to subtract fractions, finding a common denominator if necessary. For example, if one recipe calls for ½ cup butter

Teach continued

and another calls for ⅓ cup butter, you might want to see how much more butter is called for in the first recipe:

$$\frac{1}{2} - \frac{1}{3} \qquad \frac{3}{6} - \frac{2}{6} = \frac{1}{6}$$

Step 3: Guided Questions

Review the two recipes with students, then ask questions to check for understanding:

❶ How many ingredients do the two recipes have in common? (*seven*) What are they? (*flour, sugar, baking soda, baking powder, salt, eggs, vanilla*)

❷ Which recipe calls for more flour? (*muffins*)

❸ Which recipe uses more sugar? (*cupcakes*) How much more? (*¾ cup more*)

❹ Oil and margarine are both forms of shortening, or fat. How much shortening does the cupcake recipe call for? (*3 tablespoons*) How much shortening does the muffin recipe call for? (*½ cup*)

❺ If there are 8 tablespoons in ½ cup, which recipe calls for more shortening? (*muffins*)

❻ To make 36 cupcakes, how much flour will you need? (*2 ⅔ cups*)

❼ To make 36 muffins, would you need more or less than 2 cups of sugar? (*less; you would need just 1½ cups*)

❽ How much cocoa powder will you use for 36 cupcakes? (*1½ cups*)

❾ If there are 16 tablespoons to a cup, how many tablespoons of cocoa will you use? (*24 tablespoons*)

Let's Work Together

Work through the problems on the page.

Now It's Your Turn

Distribute copies of page 47 and have students work individually or in pairs to complete the *Now It's Your Turn* activity.

✳ For answers to reproducibles, see page 64.

Challenge

Cutting a Recipe
Imagine that you want to make just nine chocolate cupcakes. Rewrite the list of ingredients to show what you will need.

Name _____ Date _____

Muffins Versus Cupcakes

Choco-Banana Muffins

Makes 18 muffins
Ingredients
$1\frac{3}{4}$ cups all-purpose flour
$\frac{3}{4}$ cup sugar
1 teaspoon baking powder
1 teaspoon baking soda
$\frac{1}{2}$ teaspoon salt
1 egg
$\frac{1}{2}$ cup canola oil
$\frac{1}{2}$ cup plain nonfat yogurt
1 teaspoon vanilla extract
3 mashed ripe bananas (about 1 cup)
$\frac{3}{4}$ cup semisweet chocolate chips

Directions: Blend wet ingredients with mixer, then add dry ingredients. Pour batter into greased muffin pan and bake at 425 degrees for 20 minutes.

Cocoa-licious Cupcakes

Makes 18 cupcakes
Ingredients
$1\frac{1}{3}$ cups all-purpose flour
$\frac{1}{4}$ teaspoon baking soda
2 teaspoons baking powder
$\frac{3}{4}$ cup unsweetened cocoa powder
$\frac{1}{8}$ teaspoon salt
3 tablespoons margarine, softened
$1\frac{1}{2}$ cups white sugar
2 eggs
$\frac{3}{4}$ teaspoon vanilla extract
1 cup lowfat milk

Directions: Blend wet ingredients with mixer, then add dry ingredients. Scoop batter into greased cupcake tins. Bake in 350-degree oven for 22 minutes.

1. Which recipe calls for more flour?

   _____

   How much more? _____

2. Which recipe calls for more baking soda?

   _____

   How much more? _____

3. How many bananas will Kim need to make 36 Choco-Banana Muffins? _____

4. How much flour will Kim need to make 36 Choco-Banana Muffins? _____

5. How much salt will Daniel need to make 36 Cocoa-licious Cupcakes? _____

6. If Kim is making 36 muffins and Daniel is making 36 cupcakes, who will need more baking powder? _____

   How much more? _____

7. When Kim and Daniel check the baking supplies, they see that they have 4 teaspoons of vanilla extract. Do they have enough to make 36 muffins and 36 cupcakes, or will they need to go to the store?

   _____

8. Which recipe do you think will taste sweeter: the cupcakes or the muffins? Explain.

   _____

Key Math Formulas: When adding or subtracting fractions, be sure to change any mixed numbers to improper fractions and find a common denominator.

Building Real-Life Math Skills • © 2011 by Liane B. Onish • Scholastic Teaching Resources

Name _____ Date _____

Muffins Versus Cupcakes

Step 1

Read and compare the recipes for carrot muffins and carrot cupcakes.

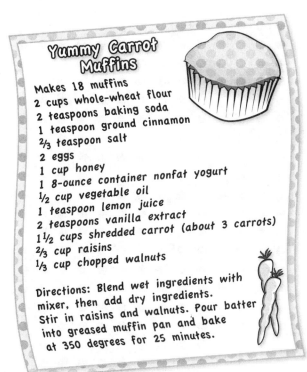

Yummy Carrot Muffins

Makes 18 muffins
2 cups whole-wheat flour
2 teaspoons baking soda
1 teaspoon ground cinnamon
2/3 teaspoon salt
2 eggs
1 cup honey
1 8-ounce container nonfat yogurt
1/2 cup vegetable oil
1 teaspoon lemon juice
2 teaspoons vanilla extract
1 1/2 cups shredded carrot (about 3 carrots)
2/3 cup raisins
1/3 cup chopped walnuts

Directions: Blend wet ingredients with mixer, then add dry ingredients. Stir in raisins and walnuts. Pour batter into greased muffin pan and bake at 350 degrees for 25 minutes.

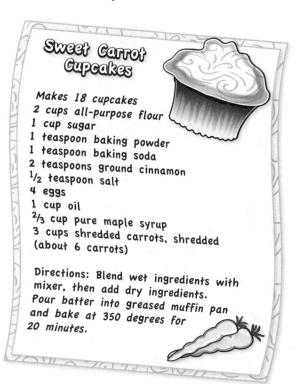

Sweet Carrot Cupcakes

Makes 18 cupcakes
2 cups all-purpose flour
1 cup sugar
1 teaspoon baking powder
1 teaspoon baking soda
2 teaspoons ground cinnamon
1/2 teaspoon salt
4 eggs
1 cup oil
2/3 cup pure maple syrup
3 cups shredded carrots, shredded (about 6 carrots)

Directions: Blend wet ingredients with mixer, then add dry ingredients. Pour batter into greased muffin pan and bake at 350 degrees for 20 minutes.

Step 2

Answer these questions.

1. Which recipe calls for more carrots?

_____

How many cups more? _____

2. Which recipe calls for more salt?

_____

How much more? _____

3. If you doubled the recipe for Yummy Carrot Muffins, how many muffins would you make? _____

4. If you doubled the recipe for Sweet Carrot Cupcakes, how much maple syrup would you need? _____

5. If you made 36 carrot muffins and 36 carrot cupcakes, how many cups of shredded carrot would you need in all?

_____

If you had a bag with 14 carrots, would you have enough? _____

6. If you made 36 carrot muffins and 36 carrot cupcakes, how much salt would you need in all? _____

7. If you wanted to make four batches of the Yummy Carrot Muffins, how many cups of raisins would you need? _____

8. If you wanted to make only half a batch of Sweet Carrot Cupcakes, how much maple syrup would you need? _____

Tracking Track

Sally's Long Jump Distances This Week

Monday	8 feet, 11 inches
Tuesday	9 feet, 7 inches
Wednesday	11 feet, 2 inches
Thursday	10 feet, 5 inches
Friday	9 feet, 8 inches

Real-Life Scenario

Sally slumped into a chair.

"Why so blue, Sally Sue?" asked her brother Sam. "Didn't you have track practice today?"

"I did. And I jumped about as far as Rex could today," she answered glumly nodding to their 9-year-old dog with a cast on his hind leg.

"Bad jumps today, great jumps tomorrow," said Sam. "You'll see."

Together they added Sally's best jump for the day to the chart she kept on the refrigerator door.

"Now let's find your average for this week," Sam said. "I bet that will make you feel better."

What's at Stake

Finding an average—and understanding that there are good days and bad days in sports training.

Teach

Step 1: Set the Stage

- Ask students to talk about what they do to keep fit. What do they measure when they are exercising? For example, it could be time, speed, or distance on a treadmill or a bike. Have volunteers share how they feel after exercising and how keeping track of time, distance, or speed helps them stay motivated.
- Talk about the math skills that will help them compare training times and average distances: adding and subtracting standard measurements and averaging.
- Read aloud the real-life scenario above.

Step 2: Overview

- Hand out copies of page 50.
- Have students list different track events they have heard of (100-yard dash, long jump, etc.). Note the key measurements used, usually time and/or distance. Point out that in U.S. track, jumps are typically measured in U.S. standard units (yards, feet, and inches) while races are now typically measured in meters.

- Review adding inches and converting to feet and inches. Remind students that there are 12 inches in a foot. Explain how to change inches to feet. For example: 8 inches + 7 inches + 3 inches = 18 inches. Another way to express this measurement is 1 foot, 6 inches.
- Review subtracting feet and inches. Remind students that they have two choices: 1) They can convert feet and inches into inches, subtract and then convert back to feet and inches. 2) Another option is to regroup, as they would in base 10, except that for each foot they rename as inches, they must add 12, not 10, to the inches column. For example:

Option 1:

   12 feet, 6 inches – 2 feet, 9 inches =
   150 inches – 33 inches = 117 inches
   (9 feet, 9 inches)

Option 2:

$$
\begin{array}{r}
{}^{11}\;\;{}^{18} \\
\cancel{12}\;\;\cancel{6}\,\text{feet, 6 inches} \\
-\;2\;\;9\,\text{feet, 9 inches} \\
\hline
9\;\;9\,\text{feet, 9 inches}
\end{array}
$$

Teach continued

- Review converting yards, feet, and inches. Have students convert the following measures in yards into feet and inches: 4 yards (12 feet = 144 inches); 5 yards, 3 inches (15 feet, 3 inches, or 183 inches).
- Review finding an average by adding the items in a list and dividing by the number of items. Have students practice with whole numbers such as test scores: 79, 87, 92, 94 (352 ÷ 4 = 88).
- Review how to find the average of multiple measurements in feet and inches. The best way is to first convert the measurements into inches by multiplying the feet by 12. Add the remaining inches. Then find the average of the measurements in inches. Convert the average back into feet and inches by dividing by 12.

Example:
Give students these distances to average:

        4 feet, 9 inches
        5 feet, 7 inches
        6 feet, 5 inches

   1. Convert into inches
      4 feet, 9 inches = 57 inches
      5 feet, 7 inches = 67 inches
      6 feet, 5 inches = 77 inches

   2. Find the average.
      57 + 67 + 77 = 201
      201 ÷ 3 = 67

   3. Convert back into feet and inches.
      67 inches = 5 feet, 7 inches

Step 3: Guided Questions

Read Sally's jump distances with students. To help them visualize the sport, point out that in the long jump, participants take a running jump onto sand. Their distance is measured from the point where the back of the heel (of the leg closest to the jumping point) hits the sand. The goal, of course, is to have the longest distance.

❶ On which day did Sally jump the farthest? How far? (*Wednesday; 11 feet, 2 inches*)

❷ How can you express her distance that day in yards, feet, and inches? (*3 yards, 2 feet, 2 inches*)

❸ Did she jump farther on Monday or on Tuesday? (*Tuesday*) How much farther? (*8 inches*)

❹ How far did she jump on Monday and Tuesday combined? (*18 feet, 6 inches*)

❺ What was her average jump on Monday and Tuesday? (*9 feet, 3 inches*)

Let's Work Together

Work through the problems on the page.

Now It's Your Turn

Distribute copies of page 51. Have students work individually or in pairs to complete the *Now It's Your Turn* activity.

✳ For answers to reproducibles, see page 64.

Challenge

My Averages

Pick something you do every day for which you can track your time or score. For example, you might keep track of how long it takes to get to school or finish your homework, how many baskets you can make in a half-hour, or even your top video game scores. Make a Monday–Friday chart and record your times or scores. Then find your average for the week.

Name _____ Date _____

Tracking Track

Sally's Long Jump Distances This Week

Monday	8 feet, 11 inches
Tuesday	9 feet, 7 inches
Wednesday	11 feet, 2 inches
Thursday	10 feet, 5 inches
Friday	9 feet, 8 inches

💡 **Remember!**
12 inches = 1 foot
3 feet = 1 yard

1. On which day did Sally take her shortest jump?
_____

   How far did she jump? _____

2. Express the distance that Sally jumped that day in inches.
_____

3. On how many days did Sally jump farther than $9\frac{1}{2}$ feet? _____

4. How far did Sally jump on Tuesday and Thursday combined?
_____

5. What was Sally's average jump distance for Tuesday and Thursday?
_____

6. What was the total distance Sally jumped on Monday, Wednesday and Friday?
_____

7. What was Sally's average jump distance on Monday, Wednesday, and Friday?
_____

8. What was Sally's average jump distance for the whole week? Round to the nearest inch.
_____

Key Math Formula: To find the average, add the items and divide by the number of items. When averaging lengths or distances, convert measurements into one unit first (in this case, inches).

Building Real-Life Math Skills • © 2011 by Liane B. Onish • Scholastic Teaching Resources

Name _____ Date _____

Tracking Track

Step 1

Sam's favorite track event is the 100-meter dash. This week, he made a chart showing his practice times. Read his chart.

Sam's 100-Meter Dash Times This Week

Monday	13.2 seconds
Tuesday	12.6 seconds
Wednesday	12.1 seconds
Thursday	13.3 seconds
Friday	11.8 seconds

Step 2

Answer these questions.

1. Which day was Sam's fastest 100-meter dash? _____

   What was his time? _____

2. Which day was Sam's slowest 100-meter dash? _____

   What was his time? _____

3. On how many days did Sam have a time faster than $12\frac{1}{2}$ seconds?

   _____

4. What was the difference between Sam's times on Tuesday and Wednesday?

   _____

5. What was his average time on Monday and Tuesday?

   _____

6. What was his average time on Wednesday and Thursday?

   _____

7. What was Sam's average time for the week?

   _____

8. If Sam wants to bring his average time to 12.0 seconds, how much time will he have to shave off his average for the week?

   _____

Happy Birthday!

Real-Life Scenario

"Have you decided how you want to celebrate your birthday?" Ryan asked his almost-10-year-old brother.

"I've narrowed it down to two kinds of parties," said Robbie. He showed Ryan the two brochures. "An ice skating party or a bowling party."

Ryan looked at the prices. "Mom and Dad's $250 budget may make the decision for you. Or you could invite fewer people."

"Would you help me figure it out?" Robbie asked.

"Sure," his brother said. "Let's look at the skating rink's brochure first."

What's at Stake

Planning a birthday party within a budget.

Teach

Step 1: Set the Stage

• Ask students to tell how they would like to celebrate their birthdays (examples: with friends at an amusement park, at a ballgame, ice skating, bowling, or on a camping trip). Then have students work with partners to guess how much a birthday party at a venue outside of home might cost.

• Talk about the math skills that will help students compute and compare party prices: money, adding, subtracting, multiplying and dividing.

• Read aloud the real-life scenario above.

Step 2: Overview

• Hand out copies of page 54.

• Discuss Robbie's two ideas: an ice skating or bowling birthday party. Point out that the ice skating option is shown on this page.

• Review what a budget is: an amount of money you have to spend for something, such as a party. Being under budget means you spend less than you had planned for. When you go over budget, you spend more than the amount you planned to spend. Discuss why going over budget is not a good idea. (*It might mean that you cannot pay for everything.*)

• Review finding per-person costs. Ask: If a party costs $120, what operation will you use to find the cost for each of 10 guests at the party? (*Divide: $120 ÷ 10 = $12*) Ask: If a party costs $240 for 12 guests, what is the per-person cost? (*$20*) Ask: If there are 15 guests at a party that costs $289, what is the approximate per-person cost? (*$19*)

• Review finding the total cost of a party when you know the cost for each guest. As you work through the following examples with students, write each total party cost on the board.

Party A: What operation will you use to find the total cost for 10 guests at a cost of $18 per person? What is the answer? (*Multiply: 10 x $18 = $180*)

Party B: What is the total cost if there are 12 guests at a party that costs $24.50 per person? (*$294*)

Party C: If there are 15 guests at a party that costs $17.50 per person, what is the total cost? (*$262.50*)

Teach continued

• Challenge students to determine whether each of the above examples fits in a budget of $250. If the party is under budget, by how much? If it is over budget, by how much? (*Party A is under budget by $70; Party B is over budget by $44; Party C is over by $12.50*)

Step 3: Guided Questions

Read the ice rink brochure with students. Then ask questions to check for understanding.

❶ How many hours of ice skating are included at a birthday party at Skate With Us Rink? (*2½*)

❷ What food item is not included, according to the brochure? (*cake*)

❸ What is the per-person price for the first 10 children? (*$17.50*)

❹ Is that greater or less than the per-person price for additional children? (*greater than*) By how much? (*$2.50*)

❺ How much would it cost to have a party for 11 people? (*$190*)

❻ How much would it cost to have a party for 18 people? (*$295*)

❼ Why do you think the rink charges a flat rate for the first 10 guests? (*Answers will vary; charging a minimum flat rate may help the rink cover its expenses or ensure a minimum profit.*)

Let's Work Together

Work through the problems on the page. Have students use a calculator if needed.

Now It's Your Turn

Distribute copies of page 55 and have students work individually or in pairs to complete the *Now It's Your Turn* activity.

✳ For answers to reproducibles, see page 64.

Challenge

Party Planning

Make a list of people (including yourself) to invite to your own ice skating party. Then calculate the cost of the party using the Skate With Us prices.

Name _____ Date _____

Happy Birthday!

Skate With Us Rink

Birthday Special Includes:

- 2 1/2 Hours of Ice Skating
- Skating Lesson With Our Party Pro
- Games on the Ice
- Pizza or Hot Dogs
- Drinks
- Party Tablecloth and Place Settings
- Balloons for the Birthday Child

Bring Your Own Birthday Cake

Cost:
$175 for the first 10 children
$15 for each additional child

---

1. How much does the rink charge for a party with only 10 children? _____

2. For a party with 10 children, what is the price per person? _____

3. How much will it cost for a party with 15 children? _____

4. For a party with 15 children, what is the approximate price per person? Round to the nearest dollar.

   _____

5. How much will it cost for a party with 17 children? _____

6. For a party with 17 children, what is the approximate price per person? Round to the nearest dollar. _____

7. If Robbie has a party at the rink for 17 children and buys a cake for $44, what will the total cost of his party be? _____

8. If Robbie has a party at the rink for 17 children and buys a cake for $44, what is the price of his party per person? _____

9. If Robbie has a budget of $250 for his party and plans on buying a $44 cake, what is the greatest number of kids he can afford to have at his party? _____

Remember! To find the total cost of a party, multiply: Price per person x the number of guests. To find the per-guest cost, divide: Total cost ÷ number of guests. When calculating party costs, don't forget to add in any extras you will need to pay for, such as cake.

Building Real-Life Math Skills • © 2011 by Liane B. Onish • Scholastic Teaching Resources

Name _____ Date _____

Happy Birthday!

Step 1

Robbie is thinking about a party at Lucky Lanes for his birthday. He has a budget of $250. Read the brochure carefully.

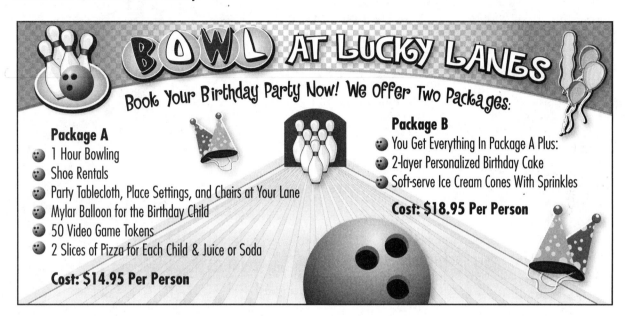

Step 2
Answer these questions.

1. How much would Package A cost for 10 children? _____

2. How much would Package B cost for 10 children? _____

3. If Robbie planned to have 15 children at his party, how much more would Package B cost than Package A? _____

4. There are 22 children in Robbie's class at school. On his $250 budget, can he afford to buy Package B and include everyone in the class? _____

5. If Robbie chooses Package A for 15 children, how much will he have left in his birthday party budget? _____

6. Cake and ice cream are included in Package B, but not in Package A. How much does Package B charge per person just for cake and ice cream? _____

7. If Robbie buys Package B for 12 children, how much would he spend on cake and ice cream? _____

   Would it be cheaper to buy his own cake and ice cream at the store for $51?

   _____

8. In the end, Robbie decides he wants to have 12 children at his party. He knows he could have a party for 12 at another local party place for $249. Will bowling Package B cost more or less than $249 for 12 children?

   _____

   How much more or less? _____

Building Real-Life Math Skills • © 2011 by Liane B. Onish • Scholastic Teaching Resources

Road Trip

Real-Life Scenario

Mayra and Mia waited while their parents got the rental car. The sisters tried to study the map, but they were so excited, it was hard to concentrate. The girls were looking forward to seeing their cousins. Every year the two families met in a U.S. national park. This year's destination was Yellowstone!

Mayra and Mia's family had flown into the Denver airport. From there they would drive to Yellowstone. Their cousins, Carl and Cam, were flying into Salt Lake City with their parents. They would drive to Yellowstone from there. The two families will meet up at Old Faithful Lodge for a week.

"When will we get there?" Mia asked, handing the map to her mom.

"Not today," answered Mom.

Mayra looked at the map. "Yellowstone is really far."

"We'll drive to Lander and stay overnight," said Dad.

"How far is Lander?" asked Mayra.

Dad handed the map to her. "Here's the map. You can figure it out."

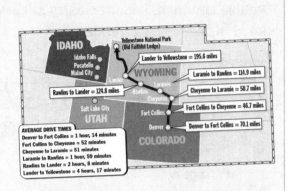

What's at Stake

Calculating the time it will take to make a long-distance drive.

Teach

Step 1: Set the Stage

- Invite students to talk about a trip they have taken with their families. Where did they go? How did they get there?
- Talk about the calculator math skills that will help them compute distance, time, and speed: adding, subtracting, multiplying, and dividing.
- Read aloud the real-life scenario above.

Step 2: Overview

- Hand out copies of page 58. Give students a few minutes to look at the map and the information below it.
- Review adding decimals. Remind students that the number to the left of the decimal is a whole number. Numbers to the right are parts of one whole. For example, 46.7 miles is

46 miles and 7/10 of a mile. Ask students how many more tenths would make the distance 47 miles (3/10). Then have them practice adding decimals with and without regrouping:

$$46.5 + 23.2 = \underline{\quad} \ (69.7)$$

$$23.3 + 14.5 = \underline{\quad} \ (37.8)$$

$$56.7 + 21.4 = \underline{\quad} \ (78.1)$$

$$29.8 + 51.4 = \underline{\quad} \ (81.2)$$

Have students check their work using calculators.

- Review adding time. Remind students to add the minutes and then convert them to hours and minutes to regroup. To convert minutes to hours, divide by 60 minutes. The remainder is extra minutes.

For example:

15 minutes + 49 minutes = 64 minutes = 1 hour, 4 minutes

Teach continued

• Have students practice adding time with these problems:

23 minutes + 48 minutes = ___ minutes = ___ hour ___ minutes (*71 minutes = 1 hour, 11 minutes*)

36 minutes + 39 minutes = ___ minutes = ___ hour ___ minutes (*75 minutes = 1 hour, 15 minutes*)

67 minutes + 56 minutes = ___ minutes = ___ hour ___ minutes (*123 minutes = 2 hours, 3 minutes*)

Have students check their work using calculators.

• Have students follow these steps to find speed in miles per hour:

— If the time is in whole hours, such as 2, then divide distance by number of hours. For example, if it took two hours to drive 110 miles, divide the distance, 110 miles, by 2 hours: 110 miles ÷ 2 hours = 55 miles per hour.

— If the time is in hours and minutes, such as 1 hour, 12 minutes:

1. Convert the hours and minutes to minutes.

2. Divide the distance by the minutes.

3. Multiply the distance per minute by 60 minutes to find distance per hour.

Example: If it takes 1 hour and 30 minutes to drive 110 miles, then:

1. Change the time to minutes: 1 hour and 30 minutes = 90 minutes

2. Divide the distance, 110 miles, by the time, 90 minutes: 110 ÷ 90 = 1.22 miles per minute

3. Multiple the distance per minute by 60 to find distance per hour: 1.22 x 60 = 73.33 miles per hour

4. Round up or down: 73.33 = about 73 miles per hour

• Then have students practice calculating speed in miles per hour (mph) with the following problems:

It took 1 hour and 15 minutes to travel 80 miles. What was the mph? (*64 mph*)

It took 2 hours and 10 minutes to travel 150 miles. What was the mph? (*69 mph*)

Step 3: Guided Questions

Study the map and mileage and time estimates with students. Then ask questions to check for understanding:

❶ How far is it from the Denver airport to Fort Collins? (*70.1 miles*)

❷ How far is it from Fort Collins to Cheyenne? (*46.7 miles*)

❸ What is the distance from the Denver airport to Cheyenne? (*116.8 miles*)

❹ How long should it take from the Denver airport to Fort Collins? (*1 hour, 14 minutes*)

❺ How long should it take from Fort Collins to Cheyenne? (*52 minutes*)

❻ How long should it take from the Denver airport to Cheyenne? (*2 hours, 6 minutes*)

❼ About how many miles per hour will the family drive from the Denver airport to Cheyenne? Round to the nearest whole number. (*about 56 mph*)

Let's Work Together

Work through the problems on the page.

Now It's Your Turn

Have students work individually or in pairs to complete the *Now It's Your Turn* activity.

✳ For answers to reproducibles, see page 64.

Challenge

From Here to There

Pick a city on the east coast and a city on the west coast. Use the Internet to find out how far apart the cities are. Then calculate how long it would take to drive from one to the other averaging 55 miles per hour.

Abbreviations Review

min = minute

hr = hour

mph = miles per hour

Name _____ Date _____

Road Trip

Remember!
1 hour = 60 minutes

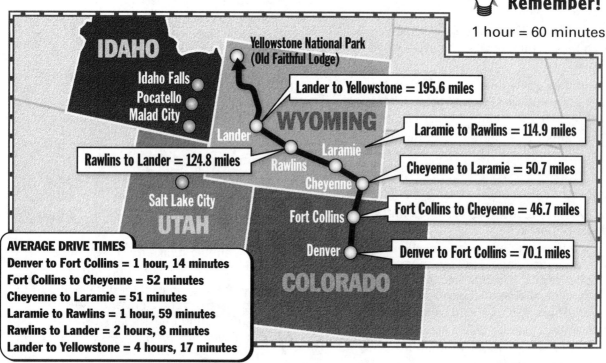

IDAHO
Idaho Falls
Pocatello
Malad City

Yellowstone National Park
(Old Faithful Lodge)

Lander to Yellowstone = 195.6 miles

WYOMING

Lander

Laramie

Laramie to Rawlins = 114.9 miles

Rawlins to Lander = 124.8 miles

Rawlins

Cheyenne to Laramie = 50.7 miles

Cheyenne

Salt Lake City

UTAH

Fort Collins

Fort Collins to Cheyenne = 46.7 miles

Denver

Denver to Fort Collins = 70.1 miles

COLORADO

AVERAGE DRIVE TIMES
Denver to Fort Collins = 1 hour, 14 minutes
Fort Collins to Cheyenne = 52 minutes
Cheyenne to Laramie = 51 minutes
Laramie to Rawlins = 1 hour, 59 minutes
Rawlins to Lander = 2 hours, 8 minutes
Lander to Yellowstone = 4 hours, 17 minutes

1. What is the distance from Cheyenne to Laramie?

_____

2. What is the distance from Laramie to Rawlins?

_____

3. What is the distance from Cheyenne to Rawlins?

_____

4. What is the drive time from Cheyenne to Rawlins?

_____

5. Given the distance and the drive time, what is the average speed (miles per hour) from Cheyenne to Rawlins? Round to the nearest whole number.

_____

6. What is the total distance from the airport in Denver to Old Faithful Lodge in Yellowstone National Park?

_____

7. What is the total time the drive should take?

_____

8. Given the distance and the time, what is the average speed (miles per hour) from the airport to Old Faithful Lodge? Round to the nearest whole number.

_____

Key Math Formulas: Follow these steps to find speed in miles per hour:

1. If time is in hours and minutes, change hours and minutes to minutes.
2. Divide distance by total number of minutes.
3. Then multiply distance per minute by 60 to find distance per hour.

Building Real-Life Math Skills • © 2011 by Liane B. Onish • Scholastic Teaching Resources

Name _____   Date _____

Road Trip

Step 1

Carl and Cam's family is driving from Salt Lake City to the Old Faithful Lodge in Yellowstone National Park. Look at the map to study their route.

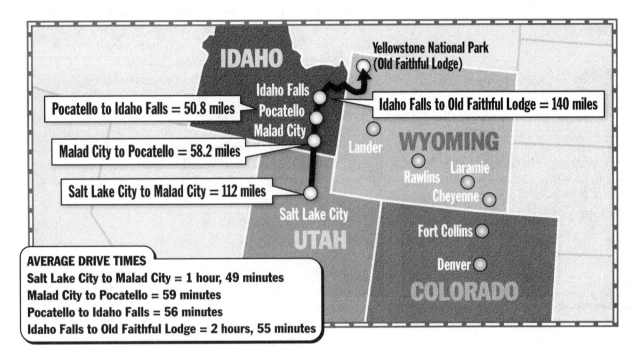

IDAHO

Yellowstone National Park (Old Faithful Lodge)

Idaho Falls
Pocatello
Malad City

Pocatello to Idaho Falls = 50.8 miles

Idaho Falls to Old Faithful Lodge = 140 miles

Lander

WYOMING

Malad City to Pocatello = 58.2 miles

Rawlins   Laramie
Cheyenne

Salt Lake City to Malad City = 112 miles

Salt Lake City

Fort Collins

UTAH

Denver

COLORADO

AVERAGE DRIVE TIMES
Salt Lake City to Malad City = 1 hour, 49 minutes
Malad City to Pocatello = 59 minutes
Pocatello to Idaho Falls = 56 minutes
Idaho Falls to Old Faithful Lodge = 2 hours, 55 minutes

Step 2

Answer the questions about Carl and Cam's trip.

1. What is the distance from Salt Lake City to Malad City?

_____

2. What is the distance from Malad City to Pocatello?

_____

3. What is the distance from Salt Lake City to Pocatello?

_____

4. What is the average drive time from Salt Lake City to Pocatello?

_____

5. Given the distance and the time, what is the average speed (miles per hour) to drive from the Salt Lake City airport to Pocatello? Round to the nearest whole number.

_____

6. What is the total distance from Salt Lake City to Old Faithful Lodge?

_____

7. What is the average drive time from Salt Lake City to Old Faithful Lodge?

_____

8. Given the distance and the time, what is the average speed (miles per hour) to drive from Salt Lake City to Old Faithful Lodge? Round to the nearest whole number.

_____

Book Fair

FOCUS SKILLS:
- Reading a tally chart   - Money
- Analyzing data

Real-Life Scenario

"Raise your hand if you want to help the Everyday Food Pantry for our community service project," said Mr. Birdwell and Ms. Dallas, the fourth-grade teachers.

Every hand shot up. "Great!" said Mr. Birdwell. "What can we do to raise money for the food pantry?"

Randy said, "Well, I have a lot of books at home that I'm done reading. What about a book fair?"

"A book fair is a great idea," said Ms. Dallas.

The next day, the fourth graders in both classes brought in books from home. Based on the condition of the books, the students priced them at $1.00, 75¢, 50¢, or 25¢. The students divided the books by genre, or type, as well as by price. They set up their book fair at recess time and made a chart to record what they sold that day.

What's at Stake

Figuring out how much money is raised for charity.

Teach

Step 1: Set the Stage

- Invite students to talk about fund-raisers or other community-service projects they have taken part in. What did they do?
- Talk about some of the math skills that people can use to track items sold during a fund-raiser: making a chart, using tally marks.
- Read aloud the real-life scenario above.

Step 2: Overview

- Hand out copies of page 61.
- Review how to read a chart. Point out that charts have headings that identify the type of information in each column or row. Guide students to notice that on the page 61 chart, the book genres are listed in the first column. The different prices are listed as headings in the remaining columns.
- Review tally markings. Explain that for each book sold, the students made a tally mark (*I*) on the chart in the correct column for the genre, and the row for the price. After four tally marks, the fifth mark is a line diagonally through the four. This makes it easy to count by fives.

Step 3: Guided Questions

Review the tally chart with students and ask questions to check for understanding.

❶ How many different genres, or types of books, did the students have for sale? (*three*)

❷ How many different prices did they sell the books for? (*four*)

❸ How much did the most expensive book cost? (*$1*) The least expensive? (*25¢*)

❹ How many sports books did the kids sell at the $1 price? (*12*) How many sports books did they sell in all? (*57*)

Let's Work Together

Work through the problems on the page.

Now It's Your Turn

Distribute copies of page 62 and have students work individually or in pairs to complete the *Now It's Your Turn* activity.

✳ For answers to reproducibles, see page 64.

Name _____   Date _____

Book Fair

Type of Book	Book Price: $1.00	Book Price: 75¢	Book Price: 50¢	Book Price: 25¢
Sports	卌 卌 卌 ||	卌 卌	卌 卌 卌	卌 卌 卌 卌
Jokes & Riddles	卌	卌 卌 ||	卌		卌 卌 卌 卌 ||
Animal Stories	卌 卌 卌	卌 卌		卌 卌 卌 卌		卌 卌 卌 卌 |||
	Total sold at this price: 32 books	Total sold at this price: _____ books	Total sold at this price: 42 books	Total sold at this price: _____ books
	Money raised from these books: $_____	Money raised from these books: $24.75	Money raised from these books: $_____	Money raised from these books: $_____

Fill in these missing totals at the bottom of the chart:

1. How much money did the students raise by selling books for $1?

2. How many books sold for 75¢ each?

3. How much money did the students raise by selling books for 50¢?

4. How many books did they sell for 25¢? How much money did they raise with those sales?

Interpret the data.

5. At what price did the students sell the most books?

_____

6. At what price did the students sell the fewest books?

_____

7. Did the students sell more sports books or animal books? _____
How many more? _____

8. What genre or type of book was most popular? _____
How much money did those books raise?

_____

9. How many books did the students sell all together? _____

10. How much money did the students raise in all? _____

Remember! A tally mark stands for one book: /
Four tally marks with a line through them stands for five books: 卌

Building Real-Life Math Skills • © 2011 by Liane B. Onish • Scholastic Teaching Resources

Now It's Your Turn

Name _____   Date _____

Book Fair

Step 1

On day two of the book fair, the fourth graders sold three more genres, or kinds, of used books. Look at the tally chart they used to track their sales.

Type of Book	Book Price: $1.00	Book Price: 75¢	Book Price: 50¢	Book Price: 25¢
Realistic Fiction	卌 卌 I	卌 卌 卌	卌 卌 I	卌 卌 II
Science Fiction	卌 卌	卌 卌	卌 卌 卌 II	卌 卌 卌 卌
Nonfiction	卌 卌 I	卌 卌 II	卌 卌 卌 III	卌 卌 卌 IIII
	Total sold at this price: 33 books	Total sold at this price: 37 books	Total sold at this price: _____ books	Total sold at this price: _____ books
	Money raised from these books: $33	Money raised from these books: $ _____	Money raised from these books: $25.50	Money raised from these books: $ _____

Step 2

First fill in these missing totals at the bottom of the chart:

1. How much money did the students raise by selling books for 75¢?

2. How many books did they sell for 50¢?

3. How many books did they sell for 25¢?

4. How much money did the students raise by selling 25¢ books?

Then answer these questions.

5. What was the best-selling genre?

_____

How many of this type did the students sell?

_____

6. At what price did the students sell the most books? _____

7. At what price did the students sell 18 nonfiction books? _____

8. How many realistic fiction books did the students sell for $1? _____

9. How many books did the students sell in all? _____

10. How much money did the students raise on day two of the book fair? _____

Building Real-Life Math Skills • © 2011 by Liane B. Onish • Scholastic Teaching Resources